Alumni Research: Methods and Applications

Gerlinda S. Melchiori, *Editor*
University of Michigan

NEW DIRECTIONS FOR INSTITUTIONAL RESEARCH

PATRICK T. TERENZINI, *Editor-in-Chief*
University of Georgia

MARVIN W. PETERSON, *Associate Editor*
University of Michigan

Number 60, Winter 1988

Paperback sourcebooks in
The Jossey-Bass Higher Education Series

Jossey-Bass Inc., Publishers
San Francisco • London

Gerlinda S. Melchiori (ed.).
Alumni Research: Methods and Applications.
New Directions for Institutional Research, no. 60.
Volume XV, Number 4.
San Francisco: Jossey-Bass, 1988.

New Directions for Institutional Research
Patrick T. Terenzini, *Editor-in-Chief*
Marvin W. Peterson, *Associate Editor*

New Directions for Institutional Research is published quarterly by
Jossey-Bass Inc., Publishers (publication number USPS 098-830), and
is sponsored by the Association for Institutional Research. The volume
and issue numbers above are included for the convenience of libraries.
Second-class postage paid at San Francisco, California, and at
additional mailing offices. POSTMASTER: Send address changes
to Jossey-Bass Inc., Publishers, 350 Sansome Street, San Francisco,
California 94104.

Editorial correspondence should be sent to the Editor-in-Chief,
Patrick T. Terenzini, Institute of Higher Education, University of
Georgia, Athens, Georgia 30602.

Library of Congress Catalog Card Number LC 85-645339

International Standard Serial Number ISSN 0271-0579

International Standard Book Number ISBN 1-55542-889-4

Cover art by WILLI BAUM

Manufactured in the United States of America. Printed on acid-free paper.

Ordering Information

The paperback sourcebooks listed below are published quarterly and can be ordered either by subscription or single copy.

Subscriptions cost $52.00 per year for institutions, agencies, and libraries. Individuals can subscribe at the special rate of $39.00 per year *if payment is by personal check*. (Note that the full rate of $52.00 applies if payment is by institutional check, even if the subscription is designated for an individual.) Standing orders are accepted.

Single copies are available at $12.95 when payment accompanies order. (California, New Jersey, New York, and Washington, D.C., residents please include appropriate sales tax.) For billed orders, cost per copy is $12.95 plus postage and handling.

Substantial discounts are offered to organizations and individuals wishing to purchase bulk quantities of Jossey-Bass sourcebooks. Please inquire.

Please note that these prices are for the calendar year 1988 and are subject to change without notice. Also, some titles may be out of print and therefore not available for sale.

To ensure correct and prompt delivery, all orders must give either the *name of an individual* or an *official purchase order number*. Please submit your order as follows:

Subscriptions: specify series and year subscription is to begin.
Single Copies: specify sourcebook code (such as, IR1) and first two words of title.

Mail orders for United States and Possessions, Latin America, Canada, Japan, Australia, and New Zealand to:
Jossey-Bass Inc., Publishers
350 Sansome Street
San Francisco, California 94104

Mail orders for all other parts of the world to:
Jossey-Bass Limited
28 Banner Street
London EC1Y 8QE

New Directions for Institutional Research Series
Patrick T. Terenzini *Editor-in-Chief*
Marvin W. Peterson, *Associate Editor*

IR1   *Evaluating Institutions for Accountability,* Howard R. Bowen
IR2   *Assessing Faculty Effort,* James I. Doi
IR3   *Toward Affirmative Action,* Lucy W. Sells

IR4   *Organizing Nontraditional Study,* Samuel Baskin
IR5   *Evaluating Statewide Boards,* Robert O. Berdahl
IR6   *Assuring Academic Progress Without Growth,* Allan M. Cartter
IR7   *Responding to Changing Human Resource Needs,* Raul Heist,
       Jonathan R. Warren
IR8   *Measuring and Increasing Academic Productivity,* Robert A. Wallhaus
IR9   *Assessing Computer-Based System Models,* Thomas R. Mason
IR10   *Examining Departmental Management,* James Smart, James Montgomery
IR11   *Allocating Resources Among Departments,* Paul L. Dressel,
       Lou Anna Kimsey Simon
IR12   *Benefiting from Interinstitutional Research,* Marvin W. Peterson
IR13   *Applying Analytic Methods to Planning and Management,*
       David S. P. Hopkins, Roger G. Scroeder
IR14   *Protecting Individual Rights to Privacy in Higher Education,*
       Alton L. Taylor
IR15   *Appraising Information Needs of Decision Makers,* Carl R. Adams
IR16   *Increasing the Public Accountability of Higher Education,* John K. Folger
IR17   *Analyzing and Constructing Cost,* Meredith A. Gonyea
IR18   *Employing Part-Time Faculty,* David W. Leslie
IR19   *Using Goals in Research and Planning,* Robert Fenske
IR20   *Evaluting Faculty Performance and Vitality,* Wayne C. Kirschling
IR21   *Developing a Total Marketing Plan,* John A. Lucas
IR22   *Examining New Trends in Administrative Computing,* E. Michael Staman
IR23   *Professional Development for Institutional Research,* Robert G. Cope
IR24   *Planning Rational Retrenchment,* Alfred L. Cooke
IR25   *The Impact of Student Financial Aid on Institutions,* Joe B. Henry
IR26   *The Autonomy of Public Colleges,* Paul L. Dressel
IR27   *Academic Program Evaluation,* Eugene C. Craven
IR28   *Academic Planning for the 1980s,* Richard B. Heydinger
IR29   *Institutional Assessment for Self-Improvement,* Richard I. Miller
IR30   *Coping with Faculty Reduction,* Stephen R. Hample
IR31   *Evaluation of Management and Planning Systems,* Nick L. Poulton
IR32   *Increasing the Use of Institutional Research,* Jack Lindquist
IR33   *Effective Planned Change Strategies,* G. Melvin Hipps
IR34   *Qualitative Methods for Institutional Research,* Eileen Kuhns,
       S. V. Martorana
IR35   *Information Technology: Innovations and Applications,* Bernard Sheehan
IR36   *Studying Student Attrition,* Ernest T. Pascarella
IR37   *Using Research for Strategic Planning,* Norman P. Uhl
IR38   *The Politics and Pragmatics of Institutional Research,* James W. Firnberg,
       William F. Lasher
IR39   *Applying Methods and Techniques of Futures Research,* James L. Morrison,
       William L. Renfro, Wayne I. Boucher
IR40   *College Faculty: Versatile Human Resources in a Period of Constraint,*
       Roger G. Baldwin, Robert T. Blackburn
IR41   *Determining the Effectiveness of Campus Services,* Robert A. Scott
IR42   *Issues in Pricing Undergraduate Education,* Larry H. Litten
IR43   *Responding to New Realities in Funding,* Larry L. Leslie
IR44   *Using Microcomputers for Planning and Management Support,*
       William L. Tetlow
IR45   *Impact and Challenges of a Changing Federal Role,*
       Virginia Ann Hodgkinson

IR46 *Institutional Research in Transition,* Marvin W. Peterson, Mary Corcoran
IR47 *Assessing Educational Outcomes,* Peter T. Ewell
IR48 *The Use of Data in Discrimination Issues Cases,* William Rosenthal, Bernard Yancey
IR49 *Applying Decision Support Systems in Higher Education,* John Rohrbaugh, Anne Taylor McCartt
IR50 *Measuring Faculty Research Performance,* John W. Creswell
IR51 *Enhancing the Management of Fund Raising,* John A. Dunn, Jr.
IR52 *Environmental Scanning for Strategic Leadership,* Patrick M. Callan
IR53 *Conducting Interinstitutional Comparisons,* Paul T. Brinkman
IR54 *Designing and Using Market Research,* Robert S. Lay, Jean J. Endo
IR55 *Managing Information in Higher Education,* E. Michael Staman
IR56 *Evaluating Administrative Services and Programs,* Jon F. Wergin, Larry A. Braskamp
IR57 *Improving Teaching and Learning Through Research,* Joan S. Stark, Lisa A. Mets
IR58 *Applying Statistics in Institutional Research,* Bernard D. Yancey
IR59 *Implementing Outcomes Assessment: Promise and Perils,* Trudy W. Banta

The Association for Institutional Research was created in 1966 to benefit, assist, and advance research leading to improved understanding, planning, and operation of institutions of higher education. Publication policy is set by its Publications Board.

For information about the Association for Institutional Research, write:

AIR Executive Office
314 Stone Building
Florida State University
Tallahassee, FL 32306-3038

(904) 644-4470

Contents

Editor's Notes   1
Gerlinda S. Melchiori

1. Alumni Research: An Introduction   5
Gerlinda S. Melchiori
As institutions increasingly turn to alumni to provide services to their alma maters in such areas as volunteering, donating, networking, and lobbying, alumni research becomes a high priority in academic administration.

2. Managing Information on Alumni   13
Kay K. Maves
At the core of any successful alumni information system is systematic and coordinated records management.

3. Surveying Your Alumni   25
Margaret Brooks Fisher
Consultation with institutional constituencies, precise operational planning and timing, and proper promotion are the crucial elements of alumni surveys.

4. Alumni Data Analysis   39
Sheryl M. Szady
Today's sophisticated computers and statistical software offer expanded opportunities for elaborate data analysis but also require careful preparation of data and thoughtful selection of analytical techniques.

5. Applying Alumni Research to Fundraising   51
Gerlinda S. Melchiori
Using empirical research methods to segment alumni markets, profile donors, prioritize prospects, and project realistic budgets becomes more important as fundraising goals expand.

6. Applying Alumni Research to Decision Making   67
Gary O. Moden, A. Michael Williford
Institutions increasingly use alumni feedback in such areas as program review, curricular planning, budget allocation, student assessment, services, and recruitment.

7. *The Future Agenda for Alumni Research*   77
John A. Dunn, Jr.

Striving for a standardized alumni research terminology should parallel future research efforts in such areas as measurement of donor potential, modeling alumni giving patterns, and examination of involvement in alumni activities.

8. *Selected References for Alumni Research*   89
Gerlinda S. Melchiori

Alumni research does not yet have its own body of literature. Therefore, further readings were selected from various related areas, such as fund-raising, marketing, survey research, and other resource books.

Index   95

Editor's Notes

If, to paraphrase Aristotle, the fate of humanity and government depends on the education of youth, institutions of learning increasingly depend on their alumni to support that goal. While this is not an entirely new situation for private institutions—certainly not for the older privates—it is very much so for public universities. In fact, the traditional view of students and graduates as being with us for only four years may very well deserve to be reviewed to reflect the continuous relationships more and more alumni have with their alma maters.

The basic purpose of this volume is to advance research on the alumni of our colleges and universities, not from a broad socioeconomic perspective but from an institutional one. We hope to validate empirical alumni research as a legitimate field of inquiry on a very important constituency of American colleges and universities, and to encourage institutional executives, especially those in development and public relations, to test its utility. After all, the need for alumni research has only been realized as more and more institutions recognize that they depend on their alumni to promote their images, build bridges to state and federal governmental agencies and to industry, bring in new students, and, most important, supplement institutional financing.

Philanthropy in higher education in 1987 reached $8.5 billion. Since alumni contributed a major portion of this total, it is understandable that institutions wish to preserve and even increase this stream of income. The more institutions know about their graduates' attitudes, life-styles, tastes, and opinions, the easier it is to cultivate a meaningful relationship with alumni.

Indeed, the utility of alumni research touches virtually all aspects of institutional operations, including program review and curriculum planning, assessment and resource allocation, student services and recruiting, volunteer activities, and fundraising. Organizationally, alumni research finds its users in all vice-presidential areas, in the president's office, and among trustees and board members. Finally, more and more state officials are listening to what alumni groups have to say about the quality and usefulness of the education they received, as those performance outcomes relate to higher education's expenditure planning on the state level.

Alumni research is appearing on many fronts now—at the Association for Institutional Research's annual forum, in the form of practica and presentations, and in the various program tracts at meetings of the Council for the Advancement and Support of Education (CASE). CASE recently hired a research director to facilitate alumni research among its

1

approximately 3,000 member institutions. Also, through a national research committee and dissertation awards, CASE is encouraging scholarly pursuits in this field. The Independent Sector, a Washington-based national forum to encourage giving, volunteering, and not-for-profit initiative, also supports this research area and has created nineteen Centers for Philanthropic Research, many of which concentrate on alumni behavior.

Who are these alumni? In Chapter One, Gerlinda S. Melchiori suggests a framework for analyzing alumni from an institutional perspective by delineating the term *alumni,* describing major subpopulations, and proposing a definition of alumni research. Considering this volume to be a small piece of a large puzzle, she concludes the chapter by alluding to some key areas of application of this research that remain to be explored.

In Chapter Two, Kay K. Maves reviews the evolution of institutional alumni recordkeeping. She describes a spectrum that includes small, manual card files, as well as complex computer networks electronically linked to the admissions office, the registrar, academic records, and the financial files. What is in these records? What should be collected? From where should the information come? She answers these questions and ends with a description of an ideal data system for alumni.

In Chapter Three, Margaret Brooks Fisher describes a survey of almost 300,000 Michigan alumni and outlines the research process from the standpoint of planning and implementation. While numerous books exist on how to do survey research in the social sciences, her emphasis is on the issues specific to alumni research. In addition, having reviewed several dozen survey instruments, she describes the elements common to most of them.

In Chapter Four, Sheryl M. Szady traces the stages of analyzing alumni survey data, from the early stage of "sums and sorts" to the later stage of fairly disaggregated analysis by units or characteristics. Particular attention is given to how empirical alumni research can lead to statistics-based market segmentation, donor profiling, and prospect ranking for identification and prioritization of alumni groups likely to volunteer services, donate funds, or perform other support activities.

Gerlinda S. Melchiori, in her role as director of the University of Michigan Census, describes in Chapter Five concepts of empirical alumni research and their application to fundraising. Moving from alumni projecting to donor profiling to prospect ranking, she concludes by using these elements as cornerstones in the strategic planning process.

Gary O. Moden and A. Michael Williford, in Chapter Six, describe the utility of alumni research in a variety of decision processes, including alumni feedback on program review and assessments, career paths, and student services and recruiting, as well as on particular colleges. The authors share their experiences in mixing general alumni-outcomes research with questions for specific colleges.

In Chapter Seven, John A. Dunn, Jr., presents one model of how to organize alumni research. He summarizes our progress in research so far and outlines some of the major components still to be pursued.

In the concluding chapter, Gerlinda S. Melchiori summarizes references and source materials for survey research, marketing, public relations, and fundraising research.

Two years ago, with his *New Directions for Institutional Research* sourcebook on fundraising, Dunn set out to build bridges between institutional research and the higher education fundraising and public relations communities. This volume demonstrates that a growing cadre of researchers and practitioners is actually crossing those bridges to bring conceptual and statistical skills together with fundraising and marketing expertise.

Gerlinda S. Melchiori
Editor

Gerlinda S. Melchiori is deputy director of the Office of Administrative Services in the University of Michigan's Office of Development. She was project director of the University of Michigan's 1986 alumni census. The authors of Chapters Two, Three, and Four were members of her project team. She currently serves on the CASE Commission on Research.

*Alumni research is proposed to focus on the role of alumni
as providers of services to their alma maters in such areas as
volunteering, donating, networking, lobbying, and mentoring.*

Alumni Research:
An Introduction

Gerlinda S. Melchiori

For decades now, institutional researchers have assisted higher education
management by analyzing outcomes, costs, and benefits of college and
university programs and by studying the behavior and attitudes of the
various constituencies, or publics, as Kotler (1975) calls them (p. 18). Of
the sixteen constituencies he lists, most of the research has focused on
students, faculty, and administrators; very little attention has been given
to research on higher education's alumni. Although alumni constitute a
social group of constantly growing importance, both in sheer numbers
and in political and financial influence, no flow charts depict their lives
and careers, no interinstitutional databases compare their outcomes.
Slowly, however, alumni research seems to have been gaining momen-
tum, and that is the thesis to be demonstrated in this chapter.

The purpose of this chapter is to describe briefly the recent evolution
of alumni research, propose working definitions of *alumni*, delineate
alumni research as a distinct area of inquiry, and summarize potential
application areas.

After the popularization of marketing research in the nonprofit sector
more than ten years ago, and its subsequent academic application (mainly
to admissions), it took threatening tax changes and an explosion of fundraising activities to spark the national interest in empirical research on

G. S. Melchiori (ed.). *Alumni Research: Methods and Applications.*
New Directions for Institutional Research, no. 60. San Francisco: Jossey-Bass, Winter 1988.

alumni, and especially on alumni giving. Research on individual alumni has occurred for some time, and specific networks and career groups have received some attention in the past, but these inquiries in no way compare to the degree of interest and methodological sophistication developed in such areas as student outcomes and faculty behavior research.

Why Such Delay?

A general explanation for the delay in alumni research may be that institutional administrators are not aware of how profoundly such research can influence operations. For example, career feedback is solicited for offices of career planning, but the results typically do not find their way back into the process of program review, curriculum planning, and central management. Alumni attitudes regarding their alma maters and their specific programs are being solicited, but the findings are not channeled back into budget allocation, student services, or any other operational service assessments.

In the past, institutions have had no concrete incentives to keep systematic track of alumni. It is not uncommon to hear of institutions that are still without records of all graduates or even information on the current addresses of living graduates. Private institutions and smaller schools in general are ahead of public institutions, especially the large ones, in tracking their graduates. At the other end of the spectrum, many community colleges have only recently joined in the pursuit of their alumni.

Many of these efforts devoted to keeping track of alumni are the results of more aggressive marketing needs for prestige, students, and additional financial resources. Today institutions are forced to look for ways to market themselves, not only to groups they hope will use their services but also to groups who can provide them with additional resources and support (Melchiori, 1984, p. 8). Alumni, then, have been discovered as a crucial marketing target, but the tasks of locating and researching them have proved difficult.

First, in a country where more than 50 percent of the population pursues higher education, the number of graduates is simply staggering. The further one tries to go back in time, the more difficult it is to identify an institution's alumni. Even if basic alumni records are reasonably complete, very little alumni information covering demographics, attitudes, and general life patterns is available over time.

Second, alumni databases typically have not enjoyed high priority in administrators' plans for expanding computer systems' capacities and enhancing their research capabilities. This is not surprising, since there has been scant institutionwide recognition of comprehensive alumni databases as gold mines for information on the kinds of impacts education has had on lives, careers, opinions, interests, and attitudes.

Third, links among central administrators, institutional researchers, and academics (typically in departments of higher education), so productive in facilitating student and faculty research, so far have not developed in alumni research. The absence of such links means that the highly specialized applications of alumni research that have evolved in fundraising, for example, have remained isolated in development departments and are undiscovered beyond. Furthermore, no national organization facilitates processes that enable institutions to do their own alumni research. There is presently no group similar to NCHEMS, for example, to offer support to alumni researchers. Nevertheless, the Council for the Advancement and Support of Education (CASE) and the Association for Institutional Research (AIR) increasingly emphasize alumni research at their conferences, with their national awards, and in their publications.

Fourth, although a few faculty members are now involved in alumni research, their preferences are for general alumni data, not institution-specific data. Massive efforts by The Independent Sector, a Washington-based national forum to encourage giving, volunteering, and not-for-profit initiative, have led so far to the creation of nineteen Centers for Philanthropic Research across the nation. It will be several more years, however, before these centers have identified their specific research agendas and begun their studies. With hardly a study now clearly postulating any theories of alumni behavior, there is great potential for such research in the near future.

Finally, because it is usually an immediate outgrowth of intense pressure to solicit additional resources, research is typically approached from the perspective of individual cases. Even if empirical research of alumni is attempted as a secondary activity, the data and the collection process often are not "clean" enough to support the standards of survey research and theory building. For instance, in fundraising, the data collected are not precise enough because researchers hesitate to ask appropriate questions clearly enough, for fear of offending alumni to the point of "turning off" potential donors.

Defining *Alumni*

Full-fledged, degree-holding alumni are relatively easy to identify—institutions are supplying various organizations annually with their numbers—but former students, or nondegree alumni, as well as the ever-present university "friends," muddy the water. *Alumni*, therefore, can be a very flexible umbrella term for various groups of people who, depending on the purpose (function or program), need identification. Three general groups can be observed.

Degree Alumni. In addition to identifying as alumni those graduates who earn bachelor's, master's, doctoral, and professional degrees, institutions individually decide whether persons who have completed certificate programs, medical residencies, postdoctoral programs, and similar activities should also be considered alumni. One would hope that such judgments would be based on the educational and philosophical principles of nationally recognized degree standards, but this is usually not the case. If a use for or an interest in this information exists, decisions are equally influenced by such procedural issues as who captures the data in what format and where, and who has access to it and for what purposes. Whatever the broader definition of *degree program* entails, institutions generally record recipients in their systems, try to maintain up-to-date address information, and report annual figures to the Council for the Advancement and Support of Education. Nationally available figures of living alumni per institution are based on these efforts.

Nondegree Alumni. In a recent survey of twenty-one institutions regarding the definitions of *alumni* and *nondegree alumni,* it was learned that a wide variety of definitions exist (Melchiori and Doke, 1987). Smaller institutions, typically private ones, are more liberal and comprehensive. They add most if not all their students who did not graduate to their alumni records. Duke University, for example, enjoys a high graduation rate, 92 percent (over five years). Thus, Duke can easily keep track of the few students per graduating class who did not finish but who would have been eligible for continued registration.

At larger institutions, the enterprise is often beyond the capacities of available staff and budgets, because of the larger number of nondegree students. It is not unusual to hear of a definition of *alumni* that requires a minimum number of credit hours, as well as the explicit expression of interest on the part of former students, before they are added to the system as alumni. In the Melchiori and Doke (1987) survey, none of the five Big Ten universities that were contacted was capturing the names and addresses of nongraduates as a matter of course. In fact, some of these institutions had discontinued the inclusion of nondegree alumni because of sheer volume, cost, and questionable utility. Public relations officers and fundraisers, in contrast, would like to have as many of these nondegree alumni as possible on their books, to enlarge both their networks and the markets from which to cultivate prospects and solicit gifts. Judgment on the cost benefits of these efforts, however, will have to be postponed until appropriate analyses are available.

Special mention should be made here of the unique problems community colleges have in defining the term *alumni.* With open-door enrollment policies on the one hand, and general feeder-institution status on the other, they are trying to identify as alumni those who, for whatever reason, have developed allegiance or loyalty to local community colleges. Since neither dropouts nor transfer students tend to develop such loyalty, one can appreciate the difficulties community colleges have in finding their alumni support groups.

Friends, or Associate Alumni. People who express interest in an institution, without having either attended or graduated, are typically accommodated in special computer segments and labeled *friends* or *associate alumni*. Some donors, although they never attended, may wish to support special activities on a campus. Parents of students or graduates may want to be identified with their children's alma mater. Individuals may want to participate in alumni club activities or obtain hard-to-get football tickets. From the institution's perspective, it may also be prudent to add to the system as friends certain community leaders, key local politicians, media people, or other prominent persons, placing them on various mailing and follow-up lists.

Defining *Alumni Research*

Although not labeled *alumni research,* several areas of research in higher education in the past have included alumni components: program review and assessment, retention research, and student outcome studies. Program review, or, in its more recent incarnation, assessment research, concerns itself with curriculum quality and appropriateness, with institutional fit, and with financial cost-benefit assessment, either in micro (department or college) or macro (region, state, or nation) contexts. Although data on the careers of alumni are solicited and are useful in the aggregate, the focus is primarily on the institution, not on the life-style and career path of the individual.

The same can be said about retention studies. Although such research compares the characteristics of alumni with those of dropouts or non-degree alumni, the purpose of these studies is to improve the institutional environment and not necessarily to learn more about the lives of those who have dropped out.

Student outcome research looks at the characteristics of newly graduated students (alumni) and relates them, for instance, to those of incoming students or previous graduates. The purpose of such research is to identify broad educational, psychological, and sociological changes or to assess the impact of higher education on its consumers. Once again, the variables of interest, for the most part, are intended as feedback to the institution for review of its academic and service functions.

A common theme of these three activities is the implicit consideration of alumni as consumers. The research results constitute "snapshots," which offer only short-term validity. This author proposes a different perspective as the focus of alumni research: alumni as long-term providers to the institution. Alumni have functioned as providers to their alma maters since the inception of higher education, as volunteers, donors, career consultants, counselors, mentors, communicators, lobbyists, and recruiters. Despite this array of services, however, only limited organized research has examined the elements of alumni as lifelong providers.

Alumni research can be defined as a process of following alumni through their lives and focusing on lifelong demographics, attitudinal issues, and career data in order to understand more fully the underlying motivational forces of alumni as providers. By isolating the characteristics that distinguish alumni as providers, research can both identify potential providers and suggest methods of stimulating provider behavior. In the past, a few characteristics have been identified and evaluated by professionals (for example, fundraisers use levels of assets to assess giving potential). Sophisticated statistical software has now made it possible to collect, weigh, and evaluate vast sets of variables and has significantly expanded the scope and purpose of alumni research.

The Uses of Alumni Research

Stiff competition for students has made it necessary to work not just with high school students but also with alumni, as parents of potential students or as potential students themselves for continuing education and career-change curricula. For the purposes of admissions networking, the differences among alumni, nondegree alumni, and friends are not of major importance. Institutions have established career-contact banks, including special networks for women and minorities, which are used to cultivate individual links to facilitate interest in programs. Career feedback is welcomed from all alumni, but especially from the successful. Finding them and identifying those who are willing to provide services are major areas of alumni research.

Moreover, institutions are in fierce competition for recognition of their accomplishments. No group is better equipped to provide prestige than alumni. The competition can be noticed on all levels. While the top institutions publicize the names of their Nobel laureates (alumni and faculty), community colleges demonstrate the extent to which their graduates fill regional professional needs. A positive image feeds back into the admissions process, helps in budget allocation, and scores nicely in the ranking business.

Further, as recent tax reforms have demonstrated, marketing via alumni also looms large in the political arena. During legislative deliberations, institutions worked through their alumni on Capitol Hill and called on their elite to represent their special interests. These efforts also revealed how unorganized and unprepared institutional marketing still is, as compared to corporate and other special-interest lobbying.

Most alumni research, however, is conducted to enhance fundraising efforts. In the past, such research has meant inquiry into the lives of individual prospects. Its results were anecdotal and descriptive reports, ranging from briefs to comprehensive profiles. While these efforts continue in ever-expanding dimensions, empirical inquiries have also begun to play a role. At first, such research came from a few academics studying philanthropy as a cultural, sociological, historical, and attitudinal phenomenon. While these areas also continue to grow, a very specific, concrete area of institution-based alumni research projects has emerged over the last few years. Conducted almost entirely for internal consumption, these projects are empirical assessments of alumni and donor characteristics for the purposes of market segmentation and strategic long-range planning. Such efforts help institutions get to know the attributes of their alumni and donors, project their potential numbers, and plan and budget accordingly.

Conclusion

The purpose of this chapter has been to define the term *alumni*, propose parameters for alumni research, and describe a few uses of such research. In principle, alumni are considered to be providers of resources, services, links, and influence. With such hopes and expectations placed on alumni, alumni research should permeate all institutional operations—academic affairs, student services, financial operations, and development—and its findings should then move into the mainstream of academic policymaking, planning, evaluating, and budgeting.

References

Kotler, P. *Marketing for Nonprofit Organizations.* Englewood Cliffs, N.J.: Prentice-Hall, 1975.

Melchiori, G. S. "Changing Public Perceptions and Expectations of Higher Education." Unpublished paper, University of Michigan, 1984.

Melchiori, G. S., and Doke, L. "Nondegree Alumni: Telephone Survey." Unpublished report, University of Michigan, 1987.

Gerlinda S. Melchiori is deputy director of the Office of Administrative Services in the University of Michigan's Office of Development. She was project director for the University of Michigan's 1986 alumni census. She currently serves on the CASE Commission on Research.

Coordinated planning and management are the critical
ingredients of any successful alumni information system.

Managing Information on Alumni

Kay K. Maves

The Current State of Information Management

Broad interest in research on alumni is a relatively recent development, but an institution's interest in alumni research may have little
relationship to its readiness to conduct the reseach. One must recognize
from the beginning that an institution's information on its alumni is the
foundation of such research efforts, and that accurate data are the basis
of any effective research. If institutional alumni records are inadequate,
productive research will be nearly impossible. This chapter addresses the
factors present in an effective records-management system and proposes
steps to create them.

Given the importance to research of proper alumni records management, it is surprising that little if any literature had addressed the subject.
This is especially true when one considers that the business community
has made a virtual science of management information systems (MIS),
and that new technologies for enhancing the management of records
emerge continually. Alumni records, like transcripts, are part of nearly
every institution's holdings, and most schools have some method for
storing the records, if not maintaining them. Yet too many institutions
remain technologically in a Dark Age. Years' worth of accumulated

G. S. Melchiori (ed.). *Alumni Research: Methods and Applications.*
New Directions for Institutional Research, no. 60. San Francisco: Jossey-Bass, Winter 1988.

paper—some of it valuable, some not—may reside in dozens of unrelated, uncoordinated files. Basic information may or may not be current. The whereabouts of most alumni may or may not be known.

Factors Influencing Successful Record Systems. Some colleges and universities do have enviable alumni record systems and use the best available technology to maintain them. Many private institutions have long traditions of records maintenance. They have depended historically on alumni, as providers not only of financial support but also of voluntary services—recruitment, mentoring, placement assistance—that expand institutional effectiveness without associated expense. Good information on alumni clearly has been necessary to these institutions' survival.

Attempting to identify effective alumni record systems by institutional sector, size, or relative prestige is a fruitless exercise, however. One cannot simply assume that if a school is large and public, its records are probably in disarray, or that small private schools will have complete information on their alumni. Interviews conducted at a recent Council for the Advancement and Support of Education conference on major-donor prospect research suggest that size, public versus private status, and relative prestige are poor indicators of the quality of an institution's data on its alumni. For example, consider the following cases.

- A well-known private college in the East reports that although its alumni are more than happy to use their alma mater's name on résumés and as a general-purpose status symbol, they are unwilling to maintain contact with the college. Because its alumni choose to ignore it, the institution has great difficulty keeping its records current.
- A small military academy in the rural Southwest maintains impressively detailed records on all its graduates on a mainframe computer system that uses sophisticated software.
- A public baccalaureate institution in the South has little information on its alumni. The president of the institution and his predecessors have placed little emphasis on alumni record maintenance, preferring instead to concentrate on finding prospective students. Two hundred miles away, another public institution, similar in size and mission, enjoys rich interaction with its alumni, who regularly provide it with fresh information on their activities.
- A large public university in the Midwest has accurate records on 90 percent of its alumni, who number more than 200,000.
- A moderate-size private university, regionally respected but without the national prestige of some of its sisters, has 55,000 alumni. Only 1,000 of them are unaccounted for, thanks primarily to institutional commitment and a dedicated staff member whose tenure extends over several decades.
- Two community colleges, one in the Midwest and the other in the

Southeast, have good alumni records. In both cases, careful monitoring of graduates by program directors provides constantly updated information.

These examples suggest that many factors beyond the traditional canons of size, sector, and prestige can contribute to a successful information system. Each of the successes noted here resulted from institutional willingness to recognize the importance of accurate information, from internal commitment to pursuing the activity, and from graduates' willingness to be tracked.

The foregoing comments are not meant to discourage institutions that are beginning to explore the potential of alumni research; rather, they are meant to offer a guide to the pragmatic obstacles that must be circumvented or overcome in planning. Every institution contends with at least some limitations, whether those already mentioned here or others, such as lack of money or staff. The initial exercises in developing an effective alumni information system are to recognize those limitations, commit the institution to overcoming them, use existing resources effectively, plan for the acquisition of additional resources, and look to the future, so that at least some of the limitations will recede or even disappear over time.

Institutional Uses of Alumni Records. Before considering the elements of effective records management, it may be useful to present a brief overview of the purposes to which record components can be put.

1. At the least, alumni records provide basic data for many purposes. Fledgling research efforts, institutional mail files, academic program follow-ups, and demographic studies are a few obvious areas of use. (The support of basic record information is so crucial to the entire system of alumni information that it is treated separately in the following pages.)

2. The inclusion of information on student activities (fraternal memberships, for example), as well as familial ties to and alumni involvement with the institution, can provide a rich body of knowledge for those who wish to identify potential volunteers or prospective donors.

3. Donor records offer support for institutional accounting and reporting and assist in the often difficult task of monitoring pledge records. Moreover, if the giving record for each donor is kept chronologically, it can be invaluable to development personnel in identifying donors' interests and major-donor prospects.

4. All available information in the record constitutes an initial resource for the production of alumni profiles, which are widely used as a tool for evaluating potential volunteers and donors prospects.

The Basic Record. Although individual institutional goals will determine the exact contents of each alumni information system, certain information is so crucial to alumni research that it forms what may be called the basic record.

The basic record on an alumnus or an alumna is the heart of the information system. It should contain a unique identifier that will link the basic record to other files, such as those maintained by the registrar and the transcript office. The most useful identifier is the social security number. Carried by each person for life, and consistently used as an identifier by government and business, it is invaluable in tracing alumni who become "lost." The basic record also should contain current and former names, current address (home, business, and possibly seasonal addresses), business title, phone number(s), spouse's name, birth date, degree(s), and major field(s) of study.

Other types of information also may be placed in the basic record, depending on institutional need. Codes that indicate the individual's receptiveness to institutional contacts, brief designators of involvement with the institution (volunteer activities, donor status, and so on), donor history, and indicators of student activities are typical examples.

No matter what makes up the basic record, it should be obvious that much of its contents are subject to frequent alteration. Americans change homes, jobs, and work and marital status with stunning frequency, and so much of the information most crucial to the maintenance of accurate records is also most liable to be inaccurate. When the information is incorrect, it creates traps that cause frustration (when alumni become unreachable because of bad addresses), institutional embarrassment (for example, when deceased alumni are solicited for contributions), and loss of support by alumni who are offended by such inaccuracies and demand that no further contact be initiated. It cannot be emphasized too strongly that the basic record is the foundation of all other information, and that effective research depends on the record's absolute correctness.

Because alumni often do not report changes in status or location to their alma maters, institutions use diverse methods to keep their basic records up to date. Some use simple measures, such as sending inquiry cards to relatives, or similar contacts. Others employ all or part of a complex range of options, including professional tracing services, clipping services, change-of-address vendors, and computerized searches. (These will be discussed later in this chapter.) Whatever method or combination of methods is chosen, it must be applied regularly and consistently. Otherwise, effective records management is impossible.

Given good basic records, the files can be expanded to include other documents. News clippings, articles, old student records, donor-research reports, and correspondence will contribute to a more complete portrait of an individual. Important as these items are, however, they must be seen as appendages to the basic record. Without the basic record, they are interesting but useless.

Defining Effective Records Management. Effective records management is characterized by the following physical conditions. All needed information on alumni is at hand and is housed in a single location. Records are organized both internally (within each individual file) and externally (within the file system as a whole), in a manner that facilitates access and maintenance. Records are free of redundant or outdated information, which contributes nothing to the completeness of the file and, indeed, may promote misinterpretation of current information.

The preceding remarks address the physical components of records; they say nothing of currency. How many records contain current information? How many alumni are "lost"? Although few institutions can boast systems that maintain current information on every one of their alumni, effective management techniques will ensure that the number of missing alumni represent only a small fraction of the whole. So managed, the record system will provide a solid foundation for ongoing research and effective planning.

Physical Management Methods

Whatever information is gathered, and whatever management style is adopted, a method of storing and retrieving the information must be chosen. Today one may elect to use traditional "hard" files, electronic files, or a combination of both.

"Hard" Files. Until recently, information managers had no choice of method. For storage, they used file cabinets, card cabinets, and even (it is rumored) shoeboxes. A number of institutions still use the file cabinet as their primary (if not sole) storage mechanism. Others maintain archival "hard" files as supplements and backup to computerized systems. Stanford University maintains a vast central archive of alumni documents, meticulously updated and cross-referenced, as a supplement to a sophisticated computer system. Yale University maintains a similar archive of extensive information on its alumni. Many institutions with relatively few alumni find that the "hard" file system is adequate and quite manageable for their needs.

However extensive any "hard" file system may be, it provides poor support for most research functions. Information of any particular complexity must be managed through what can become cumbersome cross-indexes. Moreover, the information contained in "hard" files is integrated only in the sense that all the pieces of paper concerning one individual reside in the same folder. Information contained in one document may be related to and useful in analyzing many others, but to merge related components would require cutting and pasting or manual rewriting. A "hard" file system may well be rich in information on which to base research but nearly useless because of the information's inaccessibility. Computerized summary analysis of file information is infeasible if not impossible, since conversion of data to electronic form would be a laborious and time-consuming process. Finally, "hard" files are difficult to maintain securely. If the files are accessible to many individuals, documents are likely to disappear. At the least, some will begin to deteriorate from constant handling.

Computerized Files. Computers, with their enormous capabilities, are ideally suited to managing even the largest alumni information system and to enhancing even the smallest. Twenty years ago, computer systems themselves were cumbersome enough. Today they offer speed, security, and working environments that interact with the user. They are capable of storing and retrieving documents, maintaining databases that can be linked so that information can be retrieved in any combination of components, performing statistical analyses on data, preparing tables and charts and graphs, and creating illustrated reports of typeset quality. Alumni information systems can be housed in large mainframe systems, in smaller personal computers, or in minicomputers, which are something of a compromise between the two. The choice is based largely on the number of records to be stored, the number of files to be established and linked, the anticipated uses of information, the software memory requirements and, of course, the budget.

Planning an Effective Basic System

The only effective way to ensure that a record system will meet present and future institutional needs is to plan it carefully. The following steps are crucial to successful planning.

Step 1: Secure Institutional Commitment. If top institutional officers are not already persuaded of the importance of an effective record system, they must be convinced. Remember that the expenditure of time and money on information about alumni is a relatively new practice, and that the information's long-range value for meeting institutional objectives may need to be demonstrated. A useful strategy is to present administrators with examples of the uses to which other institutions have put their alumni information systems. Include cases demonstrating the importance of an effective system to such institutional efforts as fundraising, measuring academic effectiveness, and using alumni as recruiters and institutional volunteers.

Step 2: Choose the Planners. Representatives of each office that will provide or use the system's information should participate. Apart from having needs common to all the other participants, each representative will express individual needs and concerns, based on the work of his or her office, that will affect the thinking of the other planners. Take particular care to include individuals who will be responsible for the system's day-to-day operation and maintenance. Too many systems fail because planning is conducted by top-level officials, without the advice of those who must maintain the systems.

Step 3: Determine Planning Style. Beginning with the earliest exploratory sessions, planners should be constantly reminded that each decision must rest on the premise of a system design that is flexible and expandable, in anticipation of future needs and technology. This caveat applies equally to the physical equipment used to house the system, to the software (if computers are to be used), and to the future ability of the system to accommodate new information.

Step 4: Plan. Planners must identify each piece of information necessary to support current research needs and institutional objectives. This is a pragmatic step, in which system planners examine the present and define what is needed to accomplish current objectives. Keep in mind, however, that satisfying immediate needs is only the first step, and that one must view the present in terms of the future.

All information that conceivably may be useful in the future also must be identified. This information may already be available, or it may become available as a result of new research. Whatever the case, this is the most difficult step. It is often impossible to foresee every possible need, but one must try. At the very least, planners must consider any possibility that suggests itself, no matter how unlikely it may seem. The point is not whether the need will arise, but whether the system can be expanded or adapted to meet it. By dreaming a bit, planners ensure the system's flexibility and expandability.

Step 5: Determine the Physical Form. One must balance cost against need, and against ability of alternative forms to accommodate expansion as future needs demand. Some compromise between feasibility and the ideal may be necessary. Planners under major budget constraints may agree that the ideal system would be housed in a mainframe computer and accessible from multiple terminals; yet they may settle for a minicomputer or even several microcomputers in the beginning. If the physical form of the system is chosen with flexibility and expandability in mind, however, one can begin in a relatively modest way and grow as funds become available.

Step 6: Coordinate Contribution, Maintenance, and Use. This step is crucial to current and accurate alumni information. In too many instances, inaccurate alumni information has arrived at that sorry state because too many persons have the ability to alter information. Offices frequently add or change information without coordinating their activities with other offices. In other cases, information simply is not added or changed, because no single office has been given that responsibility. It is absolutely necessary to agree on who will add the names of new graduates to the system, who will alter information in a record, who will add donor information, and even who will declare alumni deceased. The practice of allowing several offices to perform the same task should be avoided whenever possible. Perhaps the registrar will have sole authority to add the names of new graduates and provide degree information, while the alumni records office has the authority to alter addresses and phone numbers. Each office will have one capability and responsibility, but neither will be able to perform the other's function.

Planning should precede examination of existing resources, because conceiving a system around current limitations, rather than around what is desired, tends to narrow one's focus and view of the future and to impose rigidity on what should be a creative exercise.

Resource Analysis. When the preceding steps have been completed, attention can be directed to the actual analysis of existing resources. Basic central collection of data may well exist—for example, in the office of the registrar or of the alumni association—but the data may be incomplete if not out of date. The work at hand is to discover whether other, more current information is available. The questions to be answered concern what information exists, where it is, what physical form it is in, who has responsibilty for it, and how it can be obtained.

Smaller institutions may find these questions relatively easy to answer, since their potential information sources are likely to be limited to a few locations and a few responsible persons. Large institutions, and institutions that are very decentralized, may find their work more difficult. Data may be scattered among many locations, and information in one location may be contradictory to what is found in another. Information owners, fearing loss of control, may be unwilling to give data to a project that will be centralized, and a persuasive campaign may have to be mounted to secure the necessary cooperation. Whatever difficulties are encountered, however, the search must continue until all available resources are found.

In addition to investigating obvious sources of information, one should not forget other offices that routinely gather and update information. It will be wise to investigate the resources of the student loan collections office, the transcript office, and the gift-processing office. These officers can greatly assist the process of augmenting and updating information. The list of possible sources of information is limited only by the imagination of the planners, who, if they represent a broad spectrum of institutional offices, will be able to provide a complete roster of potential resources.

Creating and Maintaining the System. After alumni data have been captured, they must be brought up to date, and methods must be devised to keep them current. Separate routines must be developed for capturing accurate information on current alumni and on students about to graduate.

In the case of graduating students, care must be taken to solicit information that will permanently serve an identifying function. The most basic identifier is, of course, the social security number. (Ideally, it has been used as the student identification number and is therefore already in the student's record.) Other such data are the names and addresses of parents and close relatives, especially those who are also alumni.

The methods available for correcting erroneous information on current alumni may be modest or complex, inexpensive or expensive. At the least, the institution can designate an office to mail out update cards to the most recent address or to relatives of a "lost" alumnus or alumna. Telephone books can be used to determine whether an alumnus or an alumna still lives near the most recent address, and city directories can be used to locate former neighbors. Appeals can be issued in publications aimed at alumni. These should ask alumni to send in changes of information not only for themselves but also for friends who are also alumni. If there are local or regional alumni clubs, the institution can solicit information from them. If a research office on donors exists, it may be able to provide some of these resources, as well as the expertise of its staff in support of the effort.

Other methods of tracing alumni and updating records are more expensive, although most can be used discriminately to keep costs down. If the cost of lost information is considered, however, the perception of expense diminishes. Among the most common methods are the following.

1. *Regional or national clipping services.* These services supply clippings of newspaper and magazine articles on individuals identified as alumni. Computerized newspaper databases offer the same service electronically, and searches can be performed by institutional employees, via computer linkups, or by the service itself. The University of Michigan uses a computerized service that searches such databases for obituaries of alumni.

2. *Address-correction service.* This option is supplied by the U.S. Postal Service. For an additional fee, as part of an institutional mailing, undeliverable mail is returned, with a forwarding address affixed.

3. *Forwarding address services offered by private vendors.* A number of companies are licensed by the U.S. Postal Service to maintain its National Change of Address database. They typically retain change of address information for up to three years, instead of for the six months that the U.S. Postal Service keeps it.

4. *Credit bureaus.* Major credit bureaus keep extensive electronic records of the current and past addresses of credit applicants. A social security number generally is required for the search. The service is especially valuable because it often captures name changes and spouses' names.

5. *Professional tracers.* Individuals skilled in tracing can be hired as internal employees or outside consultants. This alternative may be the most expensive of all, especially if the institution's tracing volume is high.

Testing the System. When the basic system is finally in place, several pilot projects should be launched to test its usefulness. These projects should involve typical kinds of uses to which the system will be put. One might attempt, for example, to identify all English majors by year of graduation, select all alumni donors to the music department, or plot the geographical locations of graduates. Such a process tests the system for completeness and flexibility. It reveals flaws in planning and exposes any problems related to missing or extraneous data. Testing may slow the implementation process, but it will repay the extra effort many times over by revealing problems that will hamper the immediate usefulness of the system or limit its ability to expand and accommodate future needs.

The Ideal System

Remembering that nothing ideal exists, one can characterize the optimal alumni information system as a logical extension of the basic system just described. Like the basic system, it is intrinsically flexible, expandable, and free of errors. It takes wing, however, on its intensively electronic design, which uses state-of-the-art computer components that can expand to accommodate future technological advances and changing programmatic needs.

It might be more accurate to define such a system as a complex of systems devoted to the total management of data and the total support of research. Data are housed, by category, in totally integrated, fully relational databases. These allow the linking of selected data elements across the system, full systemwide search capabilities, data merger, and data analysis. No item of information on an alumnus or an alumna is inaccessible, impossible to include in an analysis, or incapable of being related to other items.

The system is fed by every source that gathers information on current students, prospective students, and alumni. Links with the registrar's office will permit automatic addition of the names of new graduates. The gift-processing office will update donor information as necessary. Relevant information from the alumni association, the admissions office, the personnel office, financial operations, and the transcript office will be entered into the system. These offices may maintain specialized databases of their own; nevertheless, any entry made in a specialized system will update the alumni system automatically. As research or surveys produce new data, the system expands to receive the new information or replace old information.

Users of the system will find themselves in a friendly working environment. They will be able to ask the system questions, generate reports, edit information, and select data on as exclusive and specific a basis as they wish to, without needing extensive knowledge of the technology that supports the system. Because the system is intelligent, queries and commands can be made by users' typing on keyboard consoles, touching menu items on a screen, or issuing verbal instructions. Specific questions will trigger automatic searches of stored information, and displays of relevant information will be arrayed if the user wishes to see them. For example, a development officer requesting information about a donor prospect can also receive the names of other alumni in the prospect's immediate vicinity. Similarly, block data that document average income, average number of children, and average home value for the area can be called up along with a prospect ranking for each person. Statistical analyses can be run at a touch, and high-quality graphic displays can be produced in three-dimensional color.

The physical components of the system consist of arrays of large and small computers, terminals, and storage devices. All are linked and fully compatible. A user can gain access to any portion of the system from any location. The documents previously wedged in filing cabinets are now scanned by optical devices, and their facsimiles are recorded onto twelve-inch laser disks, each of which is capable of holding nearly three million characters. Thus captured, the documents are indexed by multiple identifiers. Should a user wish to view some or all documents pertaining to a certain alumnus or alumna, a simple command will search them out and display them on the screen. If "hard" copies are needed, they will be printed in perfect facsimiles.

Is this description a wishful fantasy? It is not. All the technological components and capabilities described are current realities. Some are in exploratory stages; others are still too costly for most institutions. In the near future, however, their full power will be readily available to nearly all potential users.

The ideal system is described in futuristic terms to illustrate a point made earlier: One cannot design a basic system within the constraints of the present. Only by considering the best of all possible worlds can one conceive a current scheme that can evolve into something more powerful, flexible, and useful in the future. As for the future itself, it is just around the corner.

Kay K. Maves is director of development information services at the University of Michigan. She served on the project team of the University of Michigan's 1986 alumni census.

*Launching an alumni survey requires consultation with many
campus constituencies, thoughtful decisions about intent
and content, careful planning of all operational procedures,
and proper promotion.*

Surveying Your Alumni

Margaret Brooks Fisher

More and more institutions, public as well as private, now realize that
strong alumni involvement in planning and funding is mandatory if their
schools, colleges, or universities are to remain vital educational centers.
To engage alumni as partners in building strong institutions, educators
and administrators must know the backgrounds of their alumni—their
interests and opinions, their familial and business affiliations, and, certainly, their current geographical locations. Since this information can
easily be housed and analyzed in databases now set up, or at least planned,
for most of today's campuses, many senior administrators would argue
that up-to-date alumni information is a continuing need. With this in
mind, many more institutions are now surveying their alumni.

Although some institutions have surveyed alumni regularly, most
have done so only sporadically, and many have never even attempted
extensive surveys. This chapter is directed to researchers who are launching alumni surveys for the first time. It will guide them through planning and implementation.

Political Considerations

The timing of an alumni survey is very important, since it is often
essential to conduct a survey in time to collect and analyze the data
before launching a specific project. This is especially crucial if an insti-

G. S. Melchiori (ed.). *Alumni Research: Methods and Applications.*
New Directions for Institutional Research, no. 60. San Francisco: Jossey-Bass, Winter 1988.

tution is planning a major fundraising campaign. Information that will help determine potential major donors and suggest a strategy for approaching them should be collected and analyzed before the beginning of the campaign. If a new alumni publication is to be designed, the news staff needs to know topics that interest alumni and formats that are appealing to them long before the publication deadline. Career research that will influence program planning must be conducted well in advance of the implementation of curricular changes. Information for program review and institutional assessment must be gathered before a school is scheduled for accreditation.

Unlike standard survey research, which is often focused on a very specific area (such as use of product, or an opinion of a candidate), alumni surveys may need to accomplish objectives for various institutional units. Even though the need for the survey may first be conceived in the alumni or public relations office, or in a unit concerned with research for long-range planning, numerous campus constituencies stand to gain from the survey and should be consulted while the project is being developed. In the early stages, top-level executives and financial officers, and perhaps trustees, must be convinced of the need for such information and persuaded to fund the project. Presentations explaining the scope of the survey, as well as careful budget outlines, need to be prepared for these individuals. Such preliminary discussions may also yield worthwhile suggestions for questions to be included in the survey instrument.

Once top-level support is granted and funding is approved, various campus constituencies must be consulted in the search for consensus on the project's direction. At a large university this audience will be deans, department heads, and senior development officers in the schools and colleges, as well as directors of admissions and career planning. In a smaller school it will be department chairs or faculty members. At this point, the scope of the content and questions of the survey instrument can be decided. Planners need to make sure that all questions have a direct usefulness or an organizational home that will use the data, and that, although the survey may have several objectives, it does not attempt to serve too many mixed purposes. For example, a census for a large university with several schools and colleges will need to use questions that apply to broad interests across units, rather than requesting highly specific responses that would relate only to special-interest groups.

Selecting the Survey Method

The first step in implementing an alumni survey is to decide on the appropriate survey method. A review of survey techniques used by other institutions is essential in making this decision. The Council for the

Advancement and Support of Education (1983) offers twenty-two sample questionnaires, as well as several articles on survey projects. Contacting peer institutions by phone will also yield helpful suggestions. Researchers can discuss the usefulness of certain questions, explain their decisions to use particular survey methods, discuss the effectiveness of their processes, and share some survey results. They may also share information about vendors or consultants. It is wise to request copies of other institutions' survey instruments, to build a sample file of questionnaires for telephone and mail surveys. An institution's instrument can then be modeled on these questionnaires, with adaptations and redesign to accommodate its own needs.

After reviewing sample questionnaires, an institution must consider the kinds of alumni information it needs, which will strongly influence the choice of survey method. To establish this method, two primary decisions need to be made: whether to poll a random sample of alumni or to conduct a census of all alumni, and whether to conduct the survey by telephone or mail. Several factors will influence these decisions.

Polls of Random Samples

Attitudinal data reflecting opinions about services, programs, and publications or scanning areas of major interest can be obtained from a random sample of alumni. Research data to establish donor and non-donor characteristics for fundraising behavioral studies may also be obtained in this manner (Carbone, 1986, p. 28). In a 1981 survey, Stanford University combined the goals of market research and behavioral analysis. Researchers surveyed samples of donors and nondonors to help formulate a segmented strategy for gift appeals that would be more cost-effective than general mailings.

Surveying a random sample is certainly less costly and time-consuming than surveying the total alumni population, and a small sample of alumni can reflect relatively accurately the opinions of the entire group. The size of the sample does not have to increase proportionally with the size of the alumni body. With a total alumni population of 200, a sample of 100 is necessary; with 5,000, a sample that yields 210 responses is adequate. Indeed, as the sample size grows, the amount of reduction in error diminishes and virtually disappears with $n > 2,000$ (see Table 1).

Table 1. Standard Errors for Percentages in a Single Sample

Sample Size	100	200	300	400	500	750	1,000	1,500	2,000
Standard Error	2.18	1.54	1.26	1.09	0.97	0.80	0.69	0.56	0.49

Tables of random numbers can be found in the appendixes of most statistics books. Computerized random-sampling routines are also available in statistical software packages, such as SAS and SPSS. In a large university, a stratified random sample, which can reflect the opinions of all schools and colleges proportionally, may be appropriate. Once the total sample number has been determined, the campus computer system can be programmed to select from the database the appropriate percentage of alumni to represent each unit. A random-sample survey can be conducted either by telephone or by mail.

Census Surveys

The periodic updating of biographical data (name, address, phone number, professional title, spouse's name), necessary to all institutions, obviously cannot be done randomly. Such information can be collected by telephone but is most accurately obtained via brief mailed questionnaires. Institutions often use this method while compiling alumni directories, which are usually produced by vendors specializing in such publications. Some institutions, such as Duke University, have begun to send questionnaires to graduating classes on a regular rotating basis—in Duke's case, every five years, in the spring before the autumn class reunion.

During the past few years, however, many institutions have planned full alumni analyses so that they could design institution-specific research, to be used in soliciting both financial support and volunteers. Biographical and attitudinal information must be collected for this purpose. Using institutional staff to conduct such research is much less costly than using outside firms, and many institutions certainly are capable of doing the necessary statistical analyses. Although an institution may spread a census over several years, because of cost and staff constraints, it may be best to collect comparative data on alumni within the same time frame (for example, income data can be compared only during the same time span). For this purpose, a census of the entire alumni body is taken during a one-year period. If an institution has few or no comparative data, a census is suggested the first time a survey is undertaken, to establish baseline information for all alumni.

Telephone Versus Mail Surveys

The size of the survey population and the timeframe in which information must be collected, coupled with an institution's budgetary boundaries, will usually determine whether the survey is conducted by telephone or by mail. The cost of conducting an alumni census at a large or medium-size institution usually dictates that it be conducted by mail.

Telephone census surveys may be feasible for smaller institutions, however. For example, Bryn Mawr surveyed its 9,695 alumnae by telephone and published a book detailing the results (Miller, 1976).

A telephone survey allows more control over who responds, probably ensures higher response rates, and can be conducted more quickly. The telephone survey will be more costly, however, because individual contact by phone requires much more staff time than mass mailing does, and some cost will be incurred in training or hiring callers. For institutions with alumni spread across the United States, the expense of long-distance calls is also a consideration. A mail survey will require printing and postage, but these are less costly than extensive long-distance calls. It will certainly take more time for responses to be returned by mail, and response rates may be lower than those from telephone surveys, but fewer staff hours will be necessary to conduct the mail survey. It is also easier to collect detailed information, such as lists of business affiliations, from a printed questionnaire.

Constructing the Survey Instruments

After the survey's purpose, scope, and method are decided, the survey instrument can be constructed. Consultation with any available survey experts in an institution's academic departments may be helpful at this point. Areas of information to be sought must be determined, and questions must be grouped accordingly. Having viewed approximately forty different survey instruments, this author proposes that a typical alumni census include sections on biographical, educational, family, and career information, recreational and civic interests, and institutional interests and opinions. (Questions in purely attitudinal surveys will vary according to the opinions sought.)

Whenever possible, structured rather than open-ended questions should be used. Respondents are much more likely to answer questions in which they have only to check a box or circle a number. Questions for which responses require the writing of only a single digit or letter are easier to answer and less costly to enter into a database. Moreover, they can be readily summarized, cross-tabulated, and compared when the survey results are analyzed (Kotler, 1983, p. 67).

It will be necessary to decide whether to construct a longer survey, allowing more depth and perhaps including sensitive questions (income range), or a shorter instrument, asking for less detail and less highly personal information. The latter will probably yield a higher response rate, but the former may provide more worthwhile data. Usually a good balance can be achieved with a four-page form, long enough to be comprehensive but concise enough to encourage prompt completion.

The intensity of an attitude or an opinion can easily be captured by letting respondents answer on a scale ranging from *very satisfied* to *very dissatisfied* or from *very effectively* to *ineffectively*. The tone may be slightly more conversational for a telephone survey. To add a human-interest dimension, comments should be encouraged. Space for comments should be left at the bottom of a printed survey, and telephone callers should be prepared to elicit comments, if necessary, and capture them, as appropriate.

A letter explaining the purpose of the survey should also be prepared. Usually this is written under the name of the president or the head of the institution. For some surveys, the letter might be from another executive, the editor of a publication, or a prominent alumni volunteer. Some institutions have even chosen to include the names and pictures of the researchers conducting the survey in the letter, but whether such personalization has a negative or positive effect on response is debatable (Rucker, 1984, pp. 902–903). For mailed surveys, this piece accompanies the questionnaire as a cover letter. Assurance of confidentiality is often given in this letter, although it may also appear elsewhere in a printed survey. In the case of a telephone survey, the letter is sent to all selected call recipients in advance of the call date. Telephone callers will also want to reassure respondents of confidentiality.

Designing the Survey Package

In a mailed survey, the esthetics and layout of the survey instrument should be carefully considered. First of all, if computer-generated basic information from the institution's database will be used, the form must be designed to accommodate it. This is expensive, but for large mailings it can save time and money, since basic record entries need to be made only for those records with changes. Greater accuracy is also ensured, for the same reason. Print vendors readily describe their capabilities for computer printing, or imaging, which is ink-jetting (a form of printing) the basic record information from a computer tape (generated by an institution's database) onto the printed survey form. Mailing labels with identification numbers can also be printed at this time. Even if imaging of basic records proves too costly, a computer-printed label, with an identification number matching the number logged on the database record, will be invaluable in identifying returns and locating records for entry updates.

Also to be considered is a questionnaire format (for mail or telephone) that allows efficient and accurate computer keying. If a vendor will be used, remember that the vendor's keying rates are based on the average number of key strokes per document, as well as on the time needed to key each document. Thus, ease of scanning and the time required to turn pages both become cost considerations. Consulting a forms analyst (a professional who specializes in designing forms that will capture information for computer entry) to structure the layout would be wise in the case of large surveys. A prepaid return envelope (first class) must also be designed for each package. Photographs and graphics that will encourage recipients to read and respond to the survey are also important. An institutional symbol or logo gives mail pieces a professional image and becomes a recognized symbol when the survey is publicized. The institution's own publications department or an outside agency may design the total package.

Production Considerations

Before the survey begins, a timetable of operations must be set, and assignments or additions of staff must be made. The time between the first draft of the survey questionnaire and the inputting of the first responses may be as little as three months for a quick random-sample telephone survey, but it is more likely to be from six months to a year, depending on the size of the project. The time until completion of the analyses will vary according to the scope of the project. Simple summations and cross-tabulations can be done as soon as the information is in the database. In-depth analyses, using multiple regression or binary splits, may take much longer. The University of Michigan continued to analyze data two years after initiating its 1986 alumni census, and Bryn Mawr published the results of its all-alumnae telephone survey after four years of research.

Staff assignments for an alumni survey will be driven by the size of the project, the timeframe, and, of course, available funding. Usually the project director will want to assemble an office committee, to help conceptualize the project as a whole, and to assume individual responsibility for specific production elements, such as drafting the questionnaire, configuring computer needs, and contacting vendors.

Decisions on Data Entry

Institutions often become bogged down in entering survey responses into their databases. Perhaps the most significant production question is: "Who will enter the survey results into the database?" There are three possible answers. Existing data-entry staff can enter responses as time permits. Although this plan is appropriate to small institutions, or to small survey samples, which can be keyed quickly, it is least desirable for large-scale surveys, because the length of time required to enter the data will greatly delay access to the information. As a second option, temporary data-entry staff can be hired and trained to key in the survey responses. Finally, an outside keypunch vendor can be hired to enter the responses. Institutions should carefully investigate which of the latter two alternatives will suit their needs. Time, cost, and availability of a reputable keypunch vendor will all be determining factors. In some cases, the cost of hiring and training new staff (with no guarantee of cost per hour of entry) may equal or exceed that of using an experienced vendor who will work for a fixed fee. Moreover, large projects require additional computer stations to be set up, and both space and cost become important factors. If costs are equal, or if the vendor costs only slightly more, timeliness and convenience certainly make hiring a vendor the best choice.

This is also the time to decide if all answers need to be keyed for database analysis. Since the cost of data entry rises with each character keyed into the system, it is wise not to enter high character-count sections that will not be sorted or tabulated via the computer system (comments, names of children, lists of business affiliations), but rather to capture them by microfilming the survey response forms. With small or random-sample survey, simply filing response forms may be the best way to retain this information.

Timelines

A timetable of operations is necessarily loose in the early stages but must become very precise as final implementation nears. Drafting the questionnaire will take one to two months, depending on the number of campus constituencies who need to review and reach consensus on the document. Once the questionnaire content is fairly well set, the campus computing center, or the staff members who manage the database, need to be consulted to ensure that the computer system has the capacity to house new variables and, later, analyze the survey data. New programs to generate computer displays may need to be written and tested before response data can be entered. Since all new programs need to be in operation by the time the first responses are returned for keying, it may be necessary to allow several months for this on larger (and perhaps older) systems.

Mail Surveys

In mail surveys, printing arrangements should be made well in advance of mailing. Mail questionnaires may be printed on campus, if facilities and timetables can accommodate this plan, or by an outside vendor. Printing done on campus can usually be worked into the print shop's schedule, if the shop is consulted a month or two before the mailing date. Outside print vendors, however, will need to be interviewed at least five months before mailing. At some institutions, large print jobs must be opened to bids, and this requirement may involve even more time. To contain costs (if there is no imaging), materials for initial and follow-up mailings should be printed at the same time. Any computer-printed imaging of basic records will need to be done by a vendor equipped to do this type of work. Such vendors are also usually prepared to handle the mailing, and although this service increases costs, efficiency in handling and the ability to stay on schedule will usually make such costs a worthwhile investment. Once a printer is selected and the questionnaire design is final, the campus mail service or the local post office must be consulted to determine final postage costs and obtain nonprofit mail permits. The printer can provide a dummy form and information on the exact size and weight of the mailing.

It is wise to send a pilot or test survey to approximately 1 percent of the intended audience three months before the initial mailing. A letter to recipients, explaining that they have been selected to pretest the final survey, should be included. It should encourage comments, as well as completion of the questionnaire. From this pilot, the clarity of the questions can be assessed. The test will also show how well the format of the document facilitates the keying of responses into the database. The timing of the mailing and the percentage of response can also be analyzed. Necessary changes in the questionnaire's content or structure, and any adjustments in the mailing schedule, can then be made before printing.

A firm print date and final mailing date should be set with the vendor two months ahead. Timing of the mailing is very important. Alumni surveys should not be sent during the summer, during the Thanksgiving or Christmas seasons, or at Easter. October and November, and January through March, are the best months for mailing. The mail class used will determine the time necessary for mailing. First-class mail travels faster than third; indeed, it suggests an importance that encourages swifter return. First-class mail will also be forwarded, if the post office has been notified of an address change, or returned if it is undeliverable. First-class mail will be received by alumni within days, and the first responses can be expected within a week. Nevertheless, a large institution conducting a census of hundreds of thousands of alumni may find it financially impossible to send out the questionnaires by first-class mail. Up to three weeks may elapse before third-class bulk mail is received, and it may be another three weeks or more before large quantities are returned. A reminder postcard, which can also serve as a "thank you" to early respondents, should be sent a week or so after alumni have received the first survey forms.

A second questionnaire should be sent to nonrespondents within three weeks to several months after the initial mailing. The timing of this mailing will depend on its size and on the method of recording returns from the earlier mailing. A small mailing (which does not need to have computer tapes pulled with addresses for imaging) can easily have a three-week follow-up. Institutions that send mailings with imaging must decide whether to enter each response into the system before pulling nonrespondents for the second mailing, or to use a special indicator to mark respondents within the system. The database must be programmed for the indicator, and responses must be handled twice (once for marking and once for keying) if this method is used; thus, it is more costly. If the computer tape to generate imaged basic information is pulled during holidays or summer months, it will be necessary to wait until after these traditional vacation periods before sending the second survey form, in order to ensure a stronger return. Depending on the survey's mailing format, this second form may be accompanied by a letter explaining that it is the second request or may simply have "Second Request" printed across the front.

Telephone Surveys

For a telephone survey, a location with a bank of telephones must be secured well in advance of the calling dates. Evenings, especially the dinner hours (6:00–8:00 P.M.), are the best times to reach respondents. In nationwide surveys, sequential groups of calls can be scheduled earlier and later for several hours to accommodate varying time zones. Each completed phone call will take five to fifteen minutes, depending on the number of questions asked. At Wake Forest University, an eighty-question survey took about fifteen minutes to complete (Council for the Advancement and Support of Education, 1983, p. 13).

At institutions that already have "phonathon" facilities, time will simply need to be scheduled. Some institutions arrange evening use of phones in campus offices, while others use local businesses (such as realtors' offices) during several evenings. The telephone survey instrument should be tested before the survey calling dates. The survey committee may wish to take on this assignment itself. Content and form, as well as timing of the survey call, can be judged during the process.

For a telephone survey, hiring and training staff (usually students) to make phone calls is often the most timely way to conduct the survey. Bryn Mawr, however, used volunteers to make survey calls to over nine thousand alumnae. Yale, in contrast, used a consulting firm to survey alumni judged to be potential major donors. Paid callers need to be hired, and volunteers need to be recruited, well in advance of the call dates. Training sessions for these groups should be held just before the survey is launched. Copies of the survey questionnaire and detailed instruction sheets should be given to each caller at these sessions and posted at each telephone station. Callers should be familiar with the survey instrument and know how much time to spend soliciting each response. Copies of appropriate opening and closing remarks should be provided for callers, who should be instructed in the precise method of recording responses on the survey questionnaires. As part of standard phone-survey etiquette, a letter announcing the time, dates, and purpose of the survey should be sent to alumni about three weeks before the telephone date(s).

Publicizing the Survey

Proper planning and careful production are crucial to the success of an alumni survey, but a third element is equally important—publicity and public relations. Unlike respondents to many public-opinion or marketing surveys, alumni have a personal stake in the outcome of the surveys to which they respond, and their cooperation will be even greater when they understand this. Maintaining ties with an alma mater, whether to participate in institutional programs or influence future attendance by children, is advantageous to many graduates. Although many alumni realize the significance of being consulted via a survey, it is also important to explain it to them well in advance of the initial mailing or telephoning, and repeatedly after mailing, to encourage the return of survey forms. It is also important for alumni to understand that providing information that reveals the institution's influence on their careers or cultural and civic activities may also help shape the future direction of the alma mater. Some institutions even find it worthwhile to offer an incentive to participate in the survey, such as a school decal, a booklet, or a free (or at least reduced-rate) copy of any alumni directory compiled from the survey.

Articles explaining a forthcoming survey should begin appearing in a variety of alumni publications one or two months before the survey. The purpose and timing of the survey should be clearly stated, and participation should be encouraged. Publications that can be used include all regular campuswide alumni newspapers and magazines, as well as smaller newsletters that go out from individual departments, schools, and colleges. Articles in local newspapers can be worthwhile for community colleges and state schools. Alumni can also be contacted through campus radio and TV stations. The University of Michigan even encouraged responses during broadcasts of football games. Calvin College (Grand Rapids, Michigan), which spread its census over several years, maintained interest by running a series of profiles of alumni respondents in its alumni magazine.

Plans for publicizing the survey results should be made early and alumni should be informed about when and where they can see this information. Calvin College continued to publish results from each survey group in its alumni magazine, and the University of Michigan published a special insert in the regular alumni newspaper.

Collecting Survey Responses

Once alumni have been contacted, an institution moves from soliciting to collecting survey responses. Responses to telephone surveys are collected and recorded immediately by staff. Daily response counts are taken each time alumni are called. Although callers are trained in advance on marking survey responses, the details in comments will vary, and these must be carefully recorded immediately after calls, while memory of the conversations is still fresh. Completed questionnaires are collected after each calling session and sent in groups to the data-entry station (either on campus or in a vendor's office).

Return envelopes for mail surveys usually are addressed either to the president of the institution or to the office conducting the survey. Provision should be made for daily collection of these returns, which may number in the thousands at the peak of a large census, and for counting and opening them before keying. If keying is done at the institution, all these activities can be performed by the same staff. If keying is done by a vendor, counting and opening can occur either at the institution or on the vendor's premises. Counts of responses opened can be tallied against counts of responses keyed, as a double check of the exact number of returns. For both mail and telephone surveys, the number of returns is periodically measured against the number of alumni surveyed, to gauge the percentage of return. Computer programs can be set up to capture this information. Institutions can expect a return of 35 percent to 60 percent on mail surveys with two mailings, and an even higher response from telephone surveys. (Bryn Mawr had an 80 percent response to its telephone survey.)

Provisions need to be made for early sharing of responses, especially such items as comments that will not be keyed into the database. Development officers will be interested in seeing returns from high-income alumni who may be strong potential donors. Admissions offices may want the names of graduates who are interested in helping with recruitment, and alumni associations may want names of people interested in alumni clubs in specific geographical areas. Since this kind of information is often contained in comments, it is helpful to sort out responses with comments (usually about one-third of the returns) for special perusal. Comments can be read by the staff members who are conducting the survey or, in the case of a large survey group, in sessions that include members from various schools and colleges or offices that have an interest in the information. In some cases, comments necessitate a response or follow up, and copies of these returns can be sent to the appropriate units for response or action. Preliminary sharing of information is valuable in demonstrating the significance of the survey data to institutional units early in the process, and in helping them decide how they can best use data as they are analyzed.

With a telephone survey, the institution controls the point at which collection of responses ceases. Data entry ends when all these responses have been entered into the system. This can be done in a scheduled period of time, with data analysis immediately following. With a mail survey, the time for closure of response collection and transition to analysis is more difficult to determine. Collecting and counting responses, as well as keying information into the system, will continue until a proper number is reached for a valid survey sample, or as long as forms continue to arrive for a full census, which seeks to capture biographical information on as many alumni as possible. Once most returns are in, however, vendors' keying services can be terminated, and the trickle of late responses can be keyed by campus staff. When data must be "dumped" from one system to another for the analysis, a decision on the appropriate transfer time must be made. With a random-sample survey, the transfer is made when the proper sample number is reached. With a full census, it will be made when returns have begun to diminish significantly. The percentage of returns should range between 35 percent and 50 percent at this point. If it is below 30 percent, a third mailing should be considered, to get enough response information to give a statistically valid picture of the survey universe.

Costs

Survey costs are determined by a number of factors. Size is certainly the first determinant. Once the size is known (an all-alumni census versus a random-sample or select-group survey) and the decision has been made to survey by mail or phone, certain costs become fixed. Postage (either first or third class) is set, as is the cost for long-distance calls. Design costs offer greater flexibility. Using an outside agency and a forms analyst for design, and an off-campus print vendor for a mail survey, are more costly plans, although such firms may be able to provide more professional survey pieces that will induce greater responses. Cosmetic choices (color, photographs, grade of paper) will still influence the costs of pieces produced entirely on campus. Choosing to use imaging will increase costs, although it may also save time and ensure greater accuracy. Hiring callers, rather than using existing staff or volunteers, will increase the cost of a telephone survey. Data-entry costs will vary, depending on whether data are entered on campus or on a vendor's premises. Survey size and timeliness must be considered in deciding on all these expenditures. All these areas must be examined in establishing the budget for a survey, and the unit undertaking the survey will probably need to request a special budget appropriation for any sizable survey project.

Conclusion

Continuous surveying of alumni for current biographical and attitudinal data is becoming a necessary and ongoing activity at numerous institutions. As one survey is ending, the next may already be under way. If a periodic census is planned, efforts to correct addresses should be increased. Timing and funding will need to be reviewed again. How much will costs increase because of growth of the alumni body, plus inflation? When is the next capital campaign planned? Such questions must be considered carefully. If later annual surveys are planned to poll chronological blocks of graduating classes, class ranges and rotations need to be determined, and a continuous process must be set in motion. Most important, perhaps, the usefulness of the analyzed data from the most recent survey must be carefully evaluated, so that future surveys of alumni are structured to capture the most complete and useful information possible.

Careful planning and timing, and a sensitive awareness of an institution's political climate, are the keys to successful surveys of alumni. Survey methods, instrument content, and data recording are equally important. Using the survey techniques and timetables outlined in this chapter, small and large public and private institutions should be able to conduct surveys that will enhance and expand their alumni research efforts.

References

Carbone, R. F. *An Agenda for Research on Fund Raising.* College Park, Md.: Clearinghouse for Research on Fund Raising, University of Maryland, 1986.

Council for the Advancement and Support of Education (CASE). *Surveying Your Alumni.* Washington, D.C.: Council for the Advancement and Support of Education, 1983.

Kotler, P. *Principles of Marketing.* Englewood Cliffs, N.J.: Prentice-Hall, 1983.

Miller, A. F. (ed.). *A College in Dispersion.* Boulder, Colo.: Westview Press, 1976.

Rucker, M. "Personalization of Mail Surveys: Too Much of a Good Thing?" *Educational and Psychological Measurement,* 1984, *44*, 893–905.

Margaret Brooks Fisher is coordinator of administrative services projects in the University of Michigan's Office of Development. She served as administrative coordinator of the university's 1986 alumni census.

Careful data preparation, selection of appropriate analytical techniques, and dissemination of findings are the bases of successful alumni data-analysis efforts.

Alumni Data Analysis

Sheryl M. Szady

After the collection of new alumni information via a survey or the compilation and organization of existing research data, the next task is analysis of the aggregated data for the benefit of the institution. Relatively powerful microcomputer systems and sophisticated statistical software allow institutional researchers to perform more elaborate data analyses than ever before. This potential is further enhanced by mainframe computers that provide the capacity and power to handle large data sets in complex statistical analyses. These expanding abilities support the escalating interest in quantitative analyses of alumni for diverse institutional sectors, such as program assessment, career placement and planning, and development.

This chapter, a primer on alumni data analysis, is by no means an exhaustive study of the subject. The chapter is divided into three components: data preparation, organization of data analysis, and dissemination of the results. Each component must be carefully conceived and executed if the statistical findings are to be appropriate and valuable to the potential users.

Data Preparation

Whether one is entering new alumni data from a survey or preparing existing data for statistical manipulations, data preparation is a major

G. S. Melchiori (ed.). *Alumni Research: Methods and Applications.*
New Directions for Institutional Research, no. 60. San Francisco: Jossey-Bass, Winter 1988.

activity in alumni data analysis. Prudent preparation of data will maximize their potential for analysis. Table 1 identifies the main components and decision points of the process.

Inputting. The first decisions to be made about data preparation occur during inputting. Before data entry, a decision must be made about coding the data for inputting. From an efficiency standpoint, numerical coding of data is superior to alphabetical coding. Key entry of numerically coded data can be accomplished with one hand, leaving the other free to handle the physical copy of the data. Moreover, numerical entry is the traditional mode of financial and accounting entry clerks. Alphabetical coding does have the advantage, at times, of making literal reading of actual data easier than if numerical coding had been entered (for example, Y/N for yes/no, rather than 1/0). In addition, the ability to code twenty-six categories with a single character field (A=1, B=2, . . . Z=26) can be an asset. This reading ease must be balanced with the knowledge that all statistical software requires numerical data for analysis. Initial numerical coding reduces the amount of recoding and translation of data. In planning the input coding, one should allow for all possible responses, without combining response categories. For example, one should differentiate between a question answered *no* and one left unanswered, with distinctive no-yes, no-response, and bad-data categories. Such specificity will give the most definition to the original input data and will allow maximum latitude for data manipulations in future analyses.

Data drawn from an established database may require numerical recoding (such as A=1, B=2, . . . Z=26) or birthdays to be shortened to birth years (6/3/1952 to 52). These data can be recoded before or after a

Table 1. Data-Preparation Components

Inputting
  Coding (numerical or alphabetical)
  Category identification
  Recoding of transfer data (before or after transfer)

Selection of data fields
  Identification number
  Character fields
  Record length

Verification, dictionaries, codebooks

Temporary recoding
  Ranges
  Combining fields
  Bad data categories

Sampling (trends or identification)

Segmentation (permanent or temporary)

download or transfer to a new data file. Considerations for recoding before the download are that external programming time and cost typically are involved, once the programming is completed it can be easily reproduced, and the data are ready for use immediately after downloading. In contrast, recoding after downloading will involve less external programming time and cost, require considerable recoding efforts and time, and need to be repeated if a download is later necessary.

Data Fields. The next step is the selection of the relevant data fields for inclusion in the data file. The file may include basic record, degree, and donor information, as well as specially gathered alumni census or survey data. It is far better to have too much data per record than to endure the difficulties of attempting to add to the record later. A unique identifier (an identification number) should be part of each record. Descriptive character fields should be minimized (for example, spouse's professional title) because they tend to be lengthy and use valuable storage space, are nonnumerical and therefore cannot be the focus of statistical analysis, and can only be listed and have little sorting potential because of nonstandard formats (if they were standardized, they could be numerically coded). The approximate length of each record can be determined by dividing the available storage or memory capacity by a healthy estimation of the potential number of alumni records. The record should be filled with the most pertinent data on a priority basis.

Verification. In any movement of data, whether into a system or into a file for a statistics package, they will need to be verified for accuracy and position. This involves checking to see that correct data (or recoded data) are in the correct position in the record for a representative number of records. This process leads naturally into writing the dictionary for the data file. A dictionary file communicates the specifications of each data field to the software: data location (by starting and ending column numbers), width, intended number of decimal places, name and category labels, and missing data values. Similar to the dictionary file task is the compilation of a codebook, which lists all coding used for each category, along with some of the data specifications.

Temporary Recoding. Once all the data have been prepared, the user can introduce additional optional recoding. Temporary ranges can be defined for continuous variables (birth year, year of graduation, total giving), without forfeit of further analysis opportunities on specific years or totals or different ranges (for example, birth years of 17, 18, 19, . . . 60, 61 recoded by decades 1910-1919, 1920-1929, . . . 1960-1969, or by age brackets 1918-1927, 1928-1937, . . . 1958-1967). Some statistics or reporting programs also limit the number of categories or the value ranges that can be processed, thus requiring that variables with numerous categories be recoded. Groups of individual variables may also warrant recoding to allow them to be combined in some procedures. For example, if units A,

B, and C were separately coded 1/0, it would be impossible to distinguish the units in a combined cross-tabulation table, because all the 1's for A, B, and C would be aggregated. If unit B were recoded to 2/0, however, and unit C to 3/0, then the variables could be combined in a distinguishable manner in a table. Before recoding, separate reports would be produced (see Table 2).

Another impetus for recoding is miscellaneous values, caused by keying or downloading errors, that are uncovered as initial frequency tables or counts are generated. These erroneous category values may be recoded in a single bad-data category. This type of category, standardized for all variables, can be deleted from computations by assigning it a "missing data" designation. Many software programs allow one or two missing-data designations per variable. These are typically assigned to bad-data, blank, or no-response categories.

Sampling. If one is using a large number of records, then sampling is the next consideration. Sampling (the selection of a smaller number of records to represent the whole population) is predicated on one's purpose. If the desired outcome of analysis is the identification of trends (such as attitudes), then an appropriate sample may be reviewed. The accuracy of the sample is directly related to the homogeneity of the total population. If the purpose of analysis is to identify specific individuals, such as potential donors or student recruiters, then the entire population should be included in the analytical process.

Segmentation. A final data-preparation consideration is the division of the alumni population for research purposes. Deans, department chairs, or development officers may call for information on a particular portion of the alumni population. Partitioning or segmenting the population, in

Table 2. Recoding

Annual Personal Income

	<$20K	$20–40K	$40–60K	$60–100K	$100–200K	$200–500K	>$500K
Unit A	8%	23%	41%	19%	6%	2%	1%

Annual Personal Income

Unit B	32%	27%	19%	15%	7%	0%	0%

Annual Personal Income

Unit C	10%	16%	28%	28%	12%	4%	2%

Annual Personal Income (After Recoding)

	<$20K	$20–40K	$40–60K	$60–100K	$100–200K	$200–500K	>$500K
Unit A	8%	23%	41%	19%	6%	2%	1%
Unit B	32%	27%	19%	15%	7%	0%	0%
Unit C	10%	16%	28%	28%	12%	4%	2%

either a permanent or a temporary manner, will result in the use of a smaller file in the analysis, with less processing time and lower costs. Permanent segmentation, or subsetting, requires additional storage memory but only one execution of the subset identification process. Temporary filtering or sorting on a particular variable needs no additional memory, but the temporary file is lost after each computing session and reconstruction procedure, and costs are incurred each time the analysis is done.

Organizing the Data Analysis

After careful data preparation comes the challenge of analysis. Although projects will follow unique lines of analytical activities, the following are proposed as potential, (although not exhaustive) building blocks of analysis: data sets, segment analysis, profiles, and ranking.

The analysis of alumni begins with a study of the global alumni population. This demographic data set is composed of univariate analyses—a series of sums and frequencies of all relevant variables—possibly accompanied by descriptive statistics. Some basic bivariate or cross-tabulation tables may be included to address anticipated data needs, demonstrate the data's potential, or whet the appetite of potential users for further data analysis. Such tables might include personal annual income by gender, occupational field by gender, and personal annual income by occupation or gender.

The Data Set. The demographic data set should be established in a standard reporting format and organized from a marketing viewpoint. The order of presentation of variables should logically reflect the interests of the consumer while also highlighting significant findings. In addition, a relevant subpopulation can be defined and included in the data set (such as all alumni who are employed or self-employed on a full-time basis) for consistent analysis of occupational field, income, donor behavior, and so on.

The standardization of the data set provides a framework for parallel comparisons of subpopulations. Identical ordering of variables facilitates side-by-side reading and comparison of all aspects of the data sets, such as comparison of the complete demographic data on the mathematics alumni to the global alumni population, men to women, older alumni to younger alumni, or bankers to builders. The standardized data set should be established as a program that can be run easily on any subset of the population by adjusting the programming statements controlling the selection of cases for the analysis. The standard data set can save considerable programming time, expedite the processing of data requests, and present the user with a single, consistent reporting format.

Segment Analysis. After the global demographic description, the alumni population is segmented for further analysis. The alumni segments are defined by affiliations with units or departments. Segments also can reflect other specific consumers of the analyses: defined development regions or states for the development office, occupational fields or academic majors for career placement and planning offices, and states or graduating years by unit for the alumni association. For each of these segments, the standard data set can be run.

Profiles. Profiling is a useful compact summary format for analysis. The global or segment population is separated on a set of mutually exclusive characteristics, possibly a product of combinations of variables. A global development profile might divide the alumni population into three segments: high-end donors (generous contributors), other donors, and nondonors. The profile document differs from the standard data-set presentation in that it includes only response percentages for a subset of the data-set variables (note that variables are in the same data-set order; see Table 3). The format facilitates comparisons of the three segments. Also included in the report is the global census population, to allow comparison of any segment to the whole. A similar profile report by unit could follow the same format, with the addition of a total unit column for comparative purposes.

Ranking. After the viewing of the alumni data as a whole, as population segments, and as profiles of comparative population segments, the next step is to rank the alumni on a particular attribute or on the poten-

Table 3. Profiles

	Unit Donors		Unit Nondonors	Unit Total	Global Census Population
Variable	High-End	Other			
Birth Date					
<1900	1.0	0.5	0.8	0.6	0.6
1900–1909	9.8	4.0	4.0	4.3	4.1
1910–1919	20.5	10.8	8.7	11.1	8.4
1920–1929	20.2	15.3	8.3	14.5	13.4
1930–1939	27.2	19.7	9.0	18.5	15.7
1940–1949	17.4	28.4	20.3	26.4	24.1
1950–1959	3.6	20.1	44.1	22.8	26.2
>1960	0.3	1.2	4.8	1.8	7.5
Annual Personal Income					
<20K	1.6	2.7	7.8	3.5	19.3
20–30K	0.6	4.1	10.3	4.9	18.4
30–40K	1.6	7.5	15.4	8.3	18.8
40–60K	5.7	23.0	32.0	23.2	21.0
60–100K	18.3	30.5	24.8	28.8	13.5
100–200K	37.5	23.4	7.3	21.8	6.6
200–500K	29.0	8.1	2.3	8.5	1.9
>500	5.7	0.7	0.1	1.0	0.2

tial to attain that attribute. What is sought is a statistical procedure to support and reinforce rational and perceived notions about behavioral potential and to identify or discover additional indicators. In the development arena, ranking alumni by potential high-end donors' behavior stirs some interest. The development community recognizes that income level is a good indicator of donors' behavior, but does a thirty-year-old alumnus or alumna with an $80,000 annual income have the same giving potential as a fifty-five-year-old or a seventy-five-year-old? There must be other relevant indicators.

One traditional approach to identifying such indicators is to select the main distinguishing attribute, find a dependent variable that indicates the attribute, define the predictor variables or independent variables, and run a multiple-regression analysis, using either a mainframe or microcomputer. (See Cohen and Cohen, 1975, and Kerlinger and Pedhazur, 1973, for a complete discussion of multiple regression.) Briefly, this procedure assigns values to each of the predictors and then sums the relevant predictor values for each alumni record. The result is a record-specific total that can be compared to the total of the model population. Each alum's potential for attaining the attribute can be assessed by the proximity of the two values.

In development, for example, the dependent variable is an indicator of high-end donor status, and the independent variables are a number of data fields that might explain the variance between alumni with high-end donor status and those without it (variables such as income, marital status, number of children, age, occupation, graduation year, type of degree, field of study, number of degrees, and children, parents, or spouses also being alumni).

The practical problem of running multivariate analyses (multiple regression, discriminating functions, analysis of covariance) on demographic or survey data is that the predictor data are best if measured on interval scales, requiring ordering and equidistant categorizing of the variables (see Andrews and others, 1973). Although such data as number of children and age are bona fide interval scales, others, like marital status, occupation, type of degree, or income (if unequal ranges are used, for example, $40–60,000, $60–100,000, $100–200,000), need to be treated differently, with each category set up as a dummy variable. The integrity of the variable is negatively affected by this treatment. In addition, multivariate analyses require that such predictors as age and graduation year not be highly correlated; such intercorrelations make interpretation of results very difficult.

One solution is to employ multiple-classification analysis (MCA; see Andrews and others, 1973). A log-linear model could also be considered. This procedure is basically a multiple-regression analysis for nominal or categorical data (marital status, occupation) that also sums predictor values for each record. MCA will resolve many problems, although it requires a large number of cases, uses a large amount of core or working memory, and will have some difficulty with highly correlated categories.

A conceptual problem in MCA is its handling of the dependent variable (in the development example, it is high-end donor status). In MCA, as in multiple regression, the attributes of the dependent variable are homogenized, without consideration to different segments of the model (high-end donor) population. For example, high-end donors of different ages may have differing characteristics. A young high-end donor may have an income of $120,000, a fifty-year-old, $80,000, and a retiree, $60,000. Differences could also occur with single, married, divorced, and widowed high-end donors. The homogenized typical high-end donor may not exist in the model population, and the application of those homogenized attributes to non–high-end donors to assess giving potential would be inappropriate and misleading.

Furthermore, the resultant sums of the predictor values for each of these different age groups could and should be very similar to one another, indicating equivalent fundraising potential, but then the predictor values will not differentiate among the age groups and their attributes for the purposes of solicitation. Likewise, the totals for the other donor populations will not distinguish among subgroups that have similar predictor values but different attributes. Effective market segmentation by subgroups, with specified predictor totals, cannot be realized with this analysis.

SEARCH, a part of the OSIRIS-IV statistical program that handles nominal or categorical data and highly correlated variables (see Sonquist, Baker, and Morgan, 1973), addresses these homogenization problems. The program produces binary splits (like a genealogical tree) that divide the population (a minimum of 1,000) into groups with similar attributes. At each split, the program assesses which binary split will most improve the predicting value (or reduce the predictive error) or the dependent variable. In the development example (see Figure 1), the first split divides the population on personal annual income at $100,000. The means ("Y" value) of the top "Child" has increased, and the lower has decreased. Essentially, this shows that the proportion of high-end donors has increased in the top group and decreased in the lower group. As the splits continue, the definition of the attributes of subgroups of high-end donors becomes more specific, and the means rise. Note that the upper branches from the lower "Child" have means approaching those at the top of the tree. Thus, SEARCH defines, and distinguishes among, a number of groups with similar means but differing attributes, a distinction that is very important when it comes to selecting fundraising strategies. This analysis allows the consumer to select a population based on a

Figure 1. Ranking Binary-Split Tree

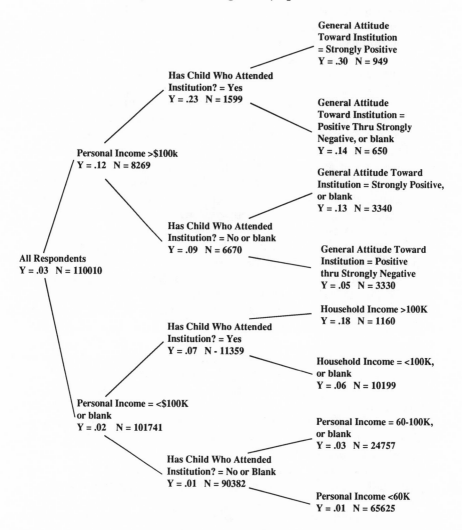

General Attitude
Toward Institution
= Strongly Positive
Y = .30 N = 949

Has Child Who Attended
Institution? = Yes
Y = .23 N = 1599

General Attitude
Toward Institution =
Positive Thru Strongly
Negative, or blank
Y = .14 N = 650

Personal Income >$100k
Y = .12 N = 8269

General Attitude Toward
Institution = Strongly Positive,
or blank
Y = .13 N = 3340

Has Child Who Attended
Institution? = No or blank
Y = .09 N = 6670

General Attitude Toward
Institution = Positive
thru Strongly Negative
Y = .05 N = 3330

All Respondents
Y = .03 N = 110010

Household Income >100K
Y = .18 N = 1160

Has Child Who Attended
Institution? = Yes
Y = .07 N - 11359

Household Income = <100K,
or blank
Y = .06 N = 10199

Personal Income = <$100K
or blank
Y = .02   N = 101741

Personal Income = 60-100K,
or blank
Y = .03 N = 24757

Has Child Who Attended
Institution? = No or Blank
Y = .01 N = 90382

Personal Income <60K
Y = .01 N = 65625

Source: The University of Michigan Office of Development (Marketing/Market Research).

mean, or according to a branch or series of branches on the binary-split tree. In addition, the grouped or ranked alumni can be sorted by unit, development region, and so on. In the development example, the non-high-end donors are the prospect portion of each group.

Dissemination of the Data Analysis

As is often the case, a large body of data can be aggregated and analyzed in the seclusion of a research office. Once the analysis is complete, however, the immediate problem is dissemination of the analysis and introduction of the user to its benefits and potential. Some of the selling of the benefits of alumni data collection is accomplished in the initial gathering of support for the project. The postanalysis challenge, however, is to organize the information in a practical and readily digestible format and distribute it in a timely fashion, without overwhelming the user.

The first task is to present the available data. A user-oriented list of variables can be compiled, with each variable identified by name and origin (from database, census, or survey), variable number, and a brief description. The order of the variables should be the same as in the standard data set. In the initial review of the list with the user, any softness in semantics or perceived discrepancies in variables should be identified—for example, misinterpretations of survey questions or discovery of variable categories that are not mutually exclusive.

Special efforts should be made to ensure that the initial data sets or analyses are presented in readily understandable and readable format. Care should be taken not to overwhelm the user with a barrage of statistical procedures or jargon. The user basically wants to know how the analyses makes him or her more effective and his or her job easier. A complex or cluttered computer-generated report will elicit an unfavorable and unfortunate evaluation, not only of the first communication but also of the alumni data analysis in general. Editing of the initial reports (in this case, the global data set) should eliminate most computer-generated statements and coding, leaving relevant information to stand alone. It is important to organize and present this report in a format similar to that of later computer-generated reports, to facilitate smooth transfer and comprehension.

The audience for alumni data analyses is twofold: alumni and internal users. If an alumni survey or, more important, an alumni census has been undertaken, then alumni participants and nonparticipants alike should receive the report of the findings, either directly or through an institutional publication. This report should reveal demographic information, both global and segmented by unit or other interest group, and should be released as soon as possible, preferably during the academic year.

The primary consumers of alumni data analysis are institutional decision makers. They can be classified by the type of information they should receive: global (community in general), unit-specific (deans and unit personnel), cross-unit comparisons (executive officers and deans), and special-focus projects, such as donor analyses (development personnel, executive officers, and deans).

Method and medium are important dissemination considerations, since they set the stage for the product. Distribution to the internal community of initial analysis materials in labeled notebooks with tabs is suggested. This tactic will underscore the importance and permanance of the analysis and promote organization, compilation, and easy identification of materials. Subsequent materials can include consecutive tabs to promote the maintenance of the research-analysis notebook.

Dissemination should coincide with perceived needs and workloads during the academic year and have a timing of its own as well. For example, the global data set at the University of Michigan (a distribution of approximately forty pages to eighty internal users) was given one week for perusal and was followed by the release of unit-specific data sets and the announcement of a briefing on the two sets of materials. Depending on the focus of the materials, general group briefings or unit briefings may be appropriate. Materials that will provoke in-depth study or planning may be strategically delayed until summer recess or other periods of lighter workload.

While the analysis of alumni data is approached in a fairly logical progression, from data preparation to analysis to dissemination, project planning should be based on the fundamental needs of the end product and its purposes. The planning of each step necessitates a focus on the next phase. Thus, while data preparation is the first step, careful planning and anticipation, combined with rigorous attention to detail and execution, will establish a solid basis for analysis. Identification of users' needs and of the goals of the research effort will assist in the establishment of the practical units, formats, and flow of analysis activities. Ultimately, as all researchers know, the presented findings are only as good as the underlying data on which they are based.

References

Andrews, F. M., Morgan, J. N., Sonquist, J. A., and Klem, L. *Multiple Classification Analysis.* (2nd ed.) Ann Arbor, Mich.: Institute for Social Research, 1973.
Cohen, J., and Cohen, P. *Applied Multiple Regression–Correlation Analysis for the Behavioral Sciences.* Hillsdale, N.J.: Erlbaum, 1975.
Kerlinger, F. N., and Pedhazur, E. J. *Multiple Regression in Behavioral Research.* New York: Holt, Rinehart & Winston, 1973.
Sonquist, J. A., Baker, E. L., and Morgan, J. N. *Searching for Structure.* (Rev. ed.) Ann Arbor, Mich.: Institute for Social Research, 1973.

Sheryl M. Szady is manager of marketing research in the University of Michigan's Office of Administrative Services. She served on the project team of the university's 1986 alumni census.

As development goals expand and the number of alumni grows, the need to use empirical research methods to segment markets, profile donors, and rank prospects will increase significantly.

Applying Alumni Research to Fundraising

Gerlinda S. Melchiori

This chapter describes methods of empirical research on alumni and suggests areas of application to fundraising. Specifically, the focus is on projecting alumni growth and its impact on program and budget planning, profiling donors and nondonors, ranking prospects, and applying all these elements to strategies for fundraising. In the current environment of constantly growing competition for charitable gifts, it is of paramount importance that fundraising executives have access to more sophisticated analyses to plan development programs, prioritize activities, and project budgets and goals.

Projecting Alumni Growth

In contrast to growth of other populations—students, faculty, staff— the number of alumni is dramatically increasing at all higher education institutions. There are simply more students graduating today than there are alumni dying. This cumulative increase is of particular interest to researchers, budget executives, and fundraising strategists, because they will find themselves rapidly dealing with an ever-eroding budget base unless they calculate the annual net increase and incorporate that addition into their programmatic and financial thinking.

G. S. Melchiori (ed.). *Alumni Research: Methods and Applications.*
New Directions for Institutional Research, no. 60. San Francisco: Jossey-Bass, Winter 1988.

Projecting the Additions. Because of the growing number of living alumni, projection models need to be developed at least as far out as the institution's long-range philanthropic programmatic planning horizon. Using ten years as an example, the growth of the first four years (two years for community colleges) can be projected relatively easily by analysis of the numbers from current enrollment figures. The remaining years can be simulated under similar enrollment policies, or by the use of projection data from the admissions office, or under assumptions of decreasing or increasing enrollment.

Projecting the Subtractions. Effective methods of identifying deceased alumni have yet to be discovered. Clearly, institutions with many communication vehicles or good networks of alumni clubs may stand a better chance of receiving death notices, obituary clippings, or nondeliverable mail. This process is still based on chance, however. A more systematic process sets default values for assumed deaths for the purpose of a projection model. For instance, anyone beyond the age of 105 could be purged from the living alumni count unless there has been activity on the record.

There are, however, two problems with this approach. Many institutions do not have age or birth date recorded for all their alumni and thus would have to default to degree year and approximate the birth date. This would be a questionable solution at best, first because age at the time of graduation varies tremendously by degree, gender, program, and so on. Second, while an institution may want an accurate count of living alumni for a variety of purposes, alumni sometimes are of interest to fundraisers well after the former have died. Recent advances in planned giving may mean that gifts from bequests, trusts, or insurance policies will not mature until years after the donor's death. Also, relatives of alumni, especially alumni who have been substantial donors, often continue the relationship with the institution, thus creating a need to retain records in the active file or the affiliated file. One approach to estimating subtractions would be to assess how many records have been moved to the inactive file over the last several years (assuming such action followed specific requests for deletion or confirmed death notices) and to project a similar trend into the future. When comparing the addition and subtraction trends thus established, most institutions will notice a net cumulative increase in their living alumni count for the long-range planning period.

Cumulative Impact of Net Increases. It seems plausible that annual increases in the number of living alumni should be recognized by top-level executives. First, such growth in alumni numbers means that the database is expanding at a fast pace, that the records offices may need more staff to input and update these files, and that "runs" off the system will become increasingly expensive. Second, it means that the institution's public relations and communication efforts, from the president's letters down to departmental curricular announcements, will require larger budget allocations to accommodate the constantly increasing volume. Third, such growth means that development offices will have built-in cost increases if they wish to include all the new alumni in their fundraising efforts. These increases initially will penetrate the broad-based annual fundraising efforts and then, over the years, will make their impact on special, major, and megadonor gift programs.

Budget and Workload Indexing. If it is well-documented, cumulative growth in the numbers of alumni suggests that annual budget allocations should increase proportionately to that growth in order to ensure, at a minimum, a steady-state development program level. Multiplying the projected number of alumni or donors by a cost-per-individual factor, one can simulate the cumulative impact that the neglect of increasing budgets would have over ten years. Development executives may want to take such simulation methods to more detailed levels. For instance, one could project when and how many of these alumni may become donors and how many in turn will become candidates for larger solicitations.

To this writer's knowledge, an actual alumni-donor flow model, such as that shown in Figure 1, has not been developed and tested. Nevertheless, institutions have good estimates of the number of alumni who become donors and, of those, the number who move into higher giving levels. Besides being able to use such estimates for workload projections, development executives may want to consider arguing for multiple budget considerations, to avoid an erosion of dollars per alumnus or donor. The first factor reflects a review of the total number of alumni and donors available for fundraising. The second consideration constitutes the typical inflation (or other cost-of-operating index) adjustment. The third factor reflects actual programmatic changes—for example, enhancements and contractions. Figure 2 displays this tripolar budget approach.

Donor Profiling

Perhaps the greatest advance in research on fundraising has occurred in the area of segmenting alumni and donors. Kotler's (1975, 1983) writ-

Figure 1. Alumni-Donor Flow

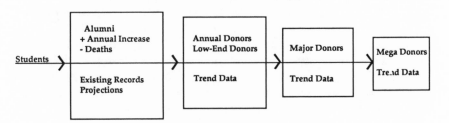

54

Figure 2. Development Budget Components

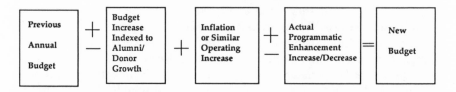

ings on marketing for the nonprofit sector have done much to convince decision makers to take a more sophisticated, corporate approach to marketing needs in higher education. For the most part, these marketing approaches have been applied to public relations and admissions. Indeed, most marketing seminars in higher education tend to focus on recruitment of students.

Still, with growing sophistication in the field of development, empirical marketing research has entered into planning and decision making. Rapid advances in the techniques of alumni and donor research, however, are hampered by several factors. First, most institutions have data systems that barely lend themselves to the production of complex reports, much less to the sorting capabilities needed for empirical research. Second, the lack of demographic and attitudinal information on alumni and donors drastically limits the variables available for analysis. Third, the lack of standards and of commonly accepted terminology in the profession makes it difficult to compare results or other benchmark information with peers. Fourth, given the financial pressures fundraisers tend to be under, their time to devote to research is limited; understandably, their attention focuses on descriptive prospect research. Finally, most development vice-presidents have not yet acquired expert staff to meet the expertise of institutional researchers who are devoted to academic affairs. Conversely, the typical institutional research office has not had enough interaction with the development department to get to know its activities, identify its research needs, and offer possible assistance. Indeed, many high consulting fees have been paid for analyses, projections, and models that could and should have been done in-house.

Donor Characteristics. Despite these limitations, progress is noticeable on two important fronts. Conceptually, a body of knowledge is evolving around the kinds of information needed to assess financial giving capability and the necessary attitudes on the part of alumni (see Paton, 1986). Second, many institutions have begun to fill such information needs through alumni surveys. Thus, the combination of existing academic records, available giving histories, and survey results is opening doors to much more comprehensive analyses. The list of variables in Figure 3 contains descriptors that the University of Michigan focused on in its research.

Figure 3. Alumni Research Variables, University of Michigan (UM)

Name
Sex
Birth date
Marital status
Number of children
State, region
Address
Spouse attended UM
Child attended UM
Parent attended UM
Annual personal income
Annual household income
Primary work status
Secondary work status
Occupational field
Business affiliation
Currently enrolled in higher education
General attitude toward UM/attitude measure
Preparation for career/satisfaction measure
Preparation for life/satisfaction measure
Degree information (#, unit, level)
Alumni association membership
Interests
    Art, business associations, charitable/political fundraising, government/
    politics, health care/hospitals, investments, libraries, local community issues,
    minority issues, museums, music, recreation/social groups, religious groups,
    theater/dance, travel, women's issues, youth service organizations,
    sports attendance, sports participation
Donor Information
    Donor, recognition levels, UM in will, last gift date, number of gifts—
    prior years, number of gift years
Student Aid Through UM
Student Involvement
    Athletics, fraternity/sorority, student government, performing groups,
    publication, honor/professional societies, special groups/clubs,
    student alumni activities
UM Interests
    Alumni programs/services, executive training programs, donor recognition
    programs, school/college fundraising, sports events, deferred giving,
    recruiting students, assisting student/career options, fundraising volunteer,
    campaign for Michigan
Information Requested (same categories as UM interests)

Figure 3. *(continued)*

Michigan Today **Readership**
　Reading frequency, topics of interest (Student life, scientific research,
　campus news, literature and art, health, university policies, sports)

Obviously, the combination of variables appropriate for institution-based
empirical alumni research is driven by institutional characteristics and
diverse elements among the alumni population, such as range of degrees,
geographical distribution, socioeconomic status, age, race, and gender, all
of which dictate the selection of variables. A strong pitch is made here for
selecting questions that most respondents can and will answer, to encourage equal response rates for all questions. For instance, in the University
of Michigan's 1986 alumni survey, practically all respondents answered
the demographic questions, while 16 percent chose not to answer the
personal-income questions, and nearly 35 percent did not answer the house-
hold-income question. As any survey researcher knows, missing data for
variables almost surely create additional work, if not problems.

　Once available, the data lend themselves to developing basic profiles
for specific alumni or donor cohorts. The first profiles assembled may be
those of universitywide annual and major donors. While this approach
may be meaningful for a homogeneous alumni body of a small private
liberal arts college, at a comprehensive research institution with a broad
degree range, the result may not appear to reveal much beyond an average to which academic units can compare themselves. Interesting distinctions may begin to emerge, however, once the data are delineated by
schools and colleges or, in some cases, by departments within a college.
Table 1 displays results from the alumni survey cited earlier. In these data
from a specific professional school, the reader will quickly notice the
differences in characteristics of major donors, other donors, nondonors,
and the census population in general. For example, the largest income
concentration of high-end donors appears in the $100,000–$200,000 category, while for other donors (anybody other than those defined as major)
the largest group appears two categories below, in the $60,000–$100,000
income range. Although this approach does not yet address the question
of interdependence among the variables selected, it does provide broad
information, easy to understand by development practitioners and appre-
ciated by deans as well.

　Usefulness of Data to Fundraisers. Table 1 presents a fairly comprehensive picture of a particular school's alumni at the University of Michigan. The major-donor profile, for instance, shows an older, 94 percent
male group with a high marriage rate and, on the average, more children.
Thus, the fundraiser has a composite view of top donors and of the kinds
of characteristics to be looked for in future prospect pools. In addition,
the profiles describe age distribution, information that can be applied to

Table 1. Donor/Nondonor Profiles
(From a University of Michigan Professional School)

Variables	Donors High-End n = 408 % 94/6	Donors Other Donors n = 6,086 % 84/16	Nondonors n = 2,765 % 82/18	Totals n = 9,389 % 84/16	Living Census Population UM TOTAL n = 11,010 % 60/40
Sex (M/F)					
Birth date					
<1900	0.3	0.0	0.1	0.1	0.6
1900–1909	2.8	0.6	0.8	0.7	4.1
1910–1919	7.3	3.8	3.2	3.7	8.4
1920–1929	23.9	13.5	13.4	13.8	13.4
1930–1939	34.7	18.3	15.6	18.0	15.7
1940–1949	25.9	25.3	21.4	23.9	24.1
1950–1959	5.0	31.5	35.7	31.8	26.2
>1960	0.3	7.0	9.9	8.1	7.5
Marital status					
Single	7.5	18.2	18.9	18.6	19.1
Married	88.3	76.6	75.7	76.3	72.1
Divorced	2.8	4.3	4.1	4.2	5.5
Widowed	1.5	0.8	1.3	1.0	3.3
Average number of children	2.78	2.45	2.44	2.46	2.48
Spouse attended UM	47.8	34.4	29.5	33.8	38.7
Children attended UM	26.7	10.1	6.0	10.0	10.6
Parent attended UM	24.5	16.0	13.5	15.7	15.4
Annual personal income					
$ <20k	1.8	4.0	6.8	5.3	19.3
20–30k	1.2	8.0	12.2	9.1	18.4
30–40k	2.7	14.3	16.7	14.6	18.8
40–60k	8.3	29.1	30.8	28.5	21.0
60–100k	23.3	25.6	22.0	24.2	13.5
100–200k	29.2	14.4	8.3	13.0	6.6
200–500k	26.8	4.1	2.7	4.5	1.9
>500k	6.8	0.6	0.5	0.8	0.3
General attitude toward UM					
Strongly positive	71.5	48.6	36.8	46.2	46.0
Positive	22.6	38.6	37.0	37.4	35.2
Slightly positive	4.1	9.4	16.5	11.2	12.7
Neutral	1.8	2.3	7.0	3.7	4.3
Slightly negative		0.6	1.6	0.9	1.0
Negative		0.3	0.9	0.5	0.5
Strongly negative		0.2	0.2	0.2	0.3

plans for deferred giving. Data on marital status, particularly if compared with data on the response group as a whole, reveal information that may warrant consideration in planning for social events (such as reunions and prospect dinners) or in composing fundraising literature. One of the big distinctions between high-end and other donors is that the former tend to have multigenerational relationships with the university, to a much larger extent than other donors.

Much has been said about the advantages and disadvantages of asking for income information in surveys. If available, however (even if only in the aggregate), wealth data are an invaluable asset. Given such data, attention can be turned to alumni who seem to have the potential of moving to higher giving levels. Supplementing income information with additional characteristics, such as work status, makes it even more powerful. Obvious differences between major and other donors are also seen in alumni attitudes toward the alma mater. Rounding out the picture are data (not included in Table 1) on interests and activities—valuable information for follow-up and contacts with specific subgroups, as well as for selecting fundraising themes, selecting newsletter content, and choosing topics for alumni get-togethers.

Ideally, the data elements underlying the profiles should be set up so that they can be aggregated into profiles in as large or as small, as generic or as specific, a manner as desirable. Deans and senior development officers will be interested in many more sorts and cohorts than researchers can anticipate. For instance, interest may focus on segmenting alumni and donors by major eras in a given college, such as before and after a curricular overhaul or a change in degree structure, to determine what impact these changes have had on attitudes and giving. Although this information does not yet provide anything close to a ranking of alumni by their giving potential and giving probability, it does introduce fundraisers to the specific sorting and subsetting potential of empirical research, as well as to its manipulation capabilities.

Prospect Ranking

One basic questions for every fundraiser is whether he or she is giving personal attention to the right people (who, of course, are those with the highest probability of giving major gifts). Surely, descriptive research, volunteers' feedback, and previous giving history are useful indicators; but what about alumni with whom the institution has had no contact? Who of the many annual donors could move to higher giving levels? The process of segmenting large groups of alumni into more finely defined prospect pools is becoming an important function of fundraising. It ranges from extensive fieldwork to alumni surveys to supplementing internal data with characteristics external to the institution (geodemographics), such as national-census demographics that provide regional socioeconomic factors like average value of home, type of car, and number of children attending private schools. Although corporate marketing has used such information for years, vendors only recently have begun to tailor it to higher education needs.

Institutions in the happy position of having information on crucial giving characteristics for a large portion of the alumni in their systems can actually develop their own in-house ranking systems. The Melchiori/ Szady ranking model, developed at the University of Michigan, was the result of a survey of all living alumni for whom the university had accurate addresses. Approximately 115,000 (46 percent) responded. For 110,010 people in this group, most of the variables already listed were available for analysis. The development of the ranking system included the following stages.

1. Transferring copies of all alumni records (name deleted), including giving history and census responses, from the administrative data system office housing the alumni/donor database to the academic mainframe computer, in order to increase statistical capacities, reduce costs, and ease direct manipulation.

2. Determining the market segment, or market group, on which to base rankings. What is the dependent variable? It was decided to focus on the characteristics of clearly defined major donors. Other groups of future interest might include consistent annual donors, persistent refusals, or sporadic donors.

3. Delineating the crucial characteristics of the focus group and determining the interdependence of these variables. While several statistical processes were evaluated, the additive model and the binary mode of analysis were scrutinized in particular. Given the size (110,010) of the population and the large number of variables, the decision was made to use SEARCH, the binary approach available within OSIRIS. (OSIRIS is a nationally available statistical software package particularly suitable to large sets of survey data.)

The decision to select major donors as a model group meant that we wished to identify all other alumni-respondents who had similar characteristics, and that we wished to rank and group them according to the strength of those characteristics. Each individual group's ranking, based on the mean value, would constitute an expression of the degree to which the individual had characteristics similar to those of this model group, as identified and ranked by the binary-tree splits. The Melchiori/Szady ranking model based on these parameters identified approximately 25,000 prospects with an above-average match of characteristics of the major-donor model group. In addition to this rather large prospect pool, another 18,000 people were identified as having a slightly less than average match of characteristics. The remaining 65,000 differed significantly from the model group. More specifically, the total number of alumni-respondents was placed in a hierarchy of twenty-nine ranks, each of which was made up of different sets of characteristics.

What did the few alumni who shared the top rank have in common? They had annual incomes of $100,000 to $200,000. Without exception, they had children who also had attended their alma mater. Almost all were male, were between sixty and eighty years old, had earned two or more degrees from the University of Michigan, and indicated very positive attitudes toward their alma mater, their careers, and life in general. They were all retired.

Plans are currently under way to use this ranking technique to segment the entire alumni-respondent spectrum, from major-gift prospects to so-called persistent refusals (see Figure 4). The envisioned total ranking scheme ranks each alumnus-respondent against a donor model group that best reflects the characteristics of the alumnus. For instance, alumni with the capability and inclination to give major gifts should be ranked at that level. Alumni whose characteristics seem to indicate that there is only a remote chance for a major gift, on the other hand, are more appropriately ranked against a different model group, such as special gift donors or annual gift donors. At the low end of the scheme, the process ranks alumni according to their probability of non-giving. The purpose of this ranking technique is to place alumni in realistic giving categories, and, by ranking them within these categories, to identify individuals with the highest probability of giving in a specific giving range.

The entire process, from surveying to modeling to ranking, should be repeated every several years. Again, it must be emphasized that these rankings are based on person-specific, not geodemographic, information. In contrast, commercially available rankings generally are based on regionally averaged national census data supplemented with household-specific information.

Usefulness of Data to Fundraisers. The major gift rank and the actual mean value can be added to each alumni-respondent record for easy reference. Thus, these indicators can become benchmarks for future reports, sorts, and lists. Their main purpose is to help rank potential prospects and easily identify their main characteristics. Prospects can now be sorted

Figure 4. Total Ranking Scheme

by schools and colleges or grouped by fundraising field-officer regions, by age for planned giving, or by interest areas. Another approach to ranking might be to group the means into quartiles, or by commonalities of the major characteristics. These ranking indicators can be used directly as selectors for specific fundraising activities (such as all upper-level giving groups for personal cultivation, and others for phone or mail solicitation), but they are also helpful in determining who deserves additional individual prospect research and who warrants immediate follow-up.

Researcher-Practitioner Interface. The issue of the interface between professional fundraisers and researchers must be given careful attention, since the degree to which information is used will depend on mutual understanding and respect. Productive cooperation between them will require several considerations.

First, to create interest and ownership in the research outcome, analysts need to make sure that practitioners join the research process, pose original questions, participate in identifying crucial characteristics of donor cohorts, and understand what the information means and what it can and cannot do. Second, researchers need to approach their communications with the development community from the programmatic end. Recommendations need to fit easily into existing departmental lines and activities, with language and terms familiar to the end consumers. Third, to avoid political interference, researchers must be aware of and understand the critical political issues prevalent in most development environments, such as the ever-present question of who has the right and access to specific alumni, or of central versus decentralized delineations regarding policy formation and budget distribution. Finally, researchers should never lose sight of the fact that their work is but a means to an end.

Applying Alumni Research to Strategic Fundraising

Planning. Even without empirical research, development professionals have been doing well in developing strategies for major fundraising efforts, and they typically conclude campaigns by surpassing their goals. If this is the case, why should institutions become more research oriented?

First, campaign goal-counting methods include some rather dubious ways to compensate for goals that have turned out to be either too high or too low. (One development professional has suggested that an analysis of "funny money" counting would make an excellent dissertation topic.) Bequests, previous pledges, and even research grants have been counted. Timeframes are shortened or lengthened as needs demand, and goals are raised if those originally set are reached too early. Clearly, there is room to develop better projection methods and standards, which may then be used across the whole spectrum of philanthropy in higher education.

Second, institutional appetites for more and more gifts have been whetted. Performance standards are constantly being raised. Presidents now expect to pursue higher goals, again requiring more comprehensive and sophisticated planning and calculating.

Third, the numbers of living alumni and donors are growing rapidly for most institutions. Therefore, development staff need to identify the most appropriate market segments and set priorities for target audiences.

Fourth, past development activities typically have been divided into major (high-end) and annual donor programs, but one can see more and more efforts to develop a wider range of programs and activities that address the special characteristics of sporadic donors, the "almost" major donors, and the ultra or megadonors. This kind of effort in turn requires the ability to segment the potential prospect pool into carefully researched subgroups.

Fifth, pockets of comparative analyses regarding cost, workload, donor-to-alumni ratios, and cost-per-dollar-raised ratios have created a cost-benefit awareness that did not exist five or ten years ago.

To further enhance and complement current planning tools (such as individual prospect identification, assessment, and ranking,) additional building blocks are suggested here.

Alumni Growth Model. As discussed before, the expected number of people available for fundraising needs to be forecast for the planning period in order to determine the overall market.

Donor Flow Model. The numbers arrived at for alumni growth need to be segmented into programmatic areas (such as annual, special, major, and megagifts), to predict the expected markets in those different programmatic environments.

Cost Analysis and Financial Planning. In the academic environment, analyses such as cost per credit hour, per student, or per class have been part of planning for many years. Fundraising operations only recently have begun to develop such cost measures. In this context, unit costs of development can be measured on a per-dollar-raised, per-alumnus, per-donor, or per-program basis, or by a combination of these factors (Dunn, 1986). Such unit measures can then be applied to projected alumni and donor growth and to institutional fundraising objectives. The relating of unit costs to projected prospects in different fundraising programs will make obvious both what the budget environment for the planning period needs to be and to what extent priority program decisions need to be made. Financial executives tend to search for economies of scale, but— with possible exceptions in the annual program areas—very few have been found. In the process of developing cost benchmarks, models and working standards can evolve that will serve fundraising executives well in long-range planning efforts. The Council for the Advancement and Support of Education/NACUBO (1986) guidelines are a good beginning in helping institutions collect and standardize their development costs.

Donor Ranking. Once programmatic goals have been established (to focus on major cash gifts, or to build up broad alumni participation, or to concentrate on enhancing pledge commitments), current and expected market segments need to be identified. If substantial information on alumni and donors is available, potential donors can be ranked by comparison of their characteristics with those of a specific model group, such as current high-end givers. The ability to select target groups from the top down in each programmatic area makes it possible to find an equilibrium between available money and reasonable expectations per program area.

Putting the Elements Together

With these elements in place, it is possible to simulate major fundraising strategies under a variety of assumptions, four of which will be mentioned here. (In reality, these strategic models appear as hybrids, rather than as separate alternatives, as described here.)

Strategic Planning Within Existing Budgets. Much planning has to occur within the confines of established budgets. Thus, the larger the expected alumni growth, the more important it is to set priorities for market segments and approach prospects who have high giving probabilities. While this planning approach may be satisfactory for well-established development programs, it is clearly not desirable for new programs that are still in the earlier stage of cultivating loyalty on the part of their alumni (preferably all their alumni).

Strategic Planning: The Incremental Model. The incremental budgetgrowth model at least represents an opportunity on the part of development vice-presidents to present fundraising potential and to argue for the most convincing of the various growth areas. Even when senior executives can afford to allocate funds quite dramatically, however, there may be constraints to expanding at too rapid a rate. The overall development infrastructure, in terms of both program and administrative support, simply may not be able to absorb rapid growth. Other concerns may include the capacities of the computer system (for gift processing), physical space, lack of a volunteer network, or alumni and prospect research that needs to be completed and analyzed first. Furthermore, it may take time to establish the proper intellectual and policy environment, before a comprehensive action program can be launched. Relatively new areas, such as corporate relations and planned giving, may serve as examples here.

Strategic Planning for Specific Goals. Determining goals for fundraising is one of the greatest challenges of developing a philanthropic strategy. Executives and deans negotiate the goals to be included in the official list of objectives. From the fundraising end, it is desirable to establish a consensus-reaching process that allows, on the one hand, ownership of the goals by the affected units and, on the other, input from fundraisers about what "sells." From the planning standpoint, this approach requires careful analysis of individual goals and of their feasibility, given a particular area and certain attitudes of prospects. The result is a careful layering of different types of goals. To the extent that empirical data on alumni interest and previous giving patterns are available, the initial market segments and interest groups can be identified and individually assessed. Caution must be exercised in determining selection criteria, so that different fundraising groups do not pursue the same people.

Strategic Planning by Potential. As institutions have worked their way through establishing a variety of fundraising offices, reached a number of goals, or even completed major campaigns, there has been a shift toward planning in more holistic frameworks and with longer time horizons. One such planning model involves starting out with a potential overall dollar goal within, say, the next five years. The larger the institution and the longer the timeframe, the more a combination of individual prospect assessment and empirical alumni research will be needed. In fact, all the building blocks already mentioned will be called on in the process. Major planning time (one to two years) is needed to complete an alumni survey, execute comprehensive prospect follow-up in the field, and investigate the capabilities and predispositions of individual prospects. Over time, the overall goal potential emerges as three types of analyses begin to approximate a similar goal figure: the empirical assessment of alumni (donor) participation, the case-by-case analysis of individual prospects or of specific development programs, and previous overall giving history simulated into the future under certain assumptions of growth. Historical trends, practitioners' best guesses, and empirical research combined are the driving forces of strategic planning.

Summary

The purpose of this chapter has been to advocate empirical research on alumni for fundraising. To demonstrate its usefulness, various elements were described and shown to fit into the development planning and decision-making processes. Empirical research was proposed as a supplement to the well-established tools of case-by-case tracking and analyzing, volunteer networking, and research on individual prospects. In long-range planning, empirical research should come first, to set general parameters. In day-to-day fundraising operations, the strength of empirical research on alumni is that it identifies market segments, sets priorities for prospects within those groups, and suggests giving potential in the absence of solid individual research. To accomplish the smooth integration of such research into both planning and actual fundraising, development executives may want to build bridges with institutional researchers or, preferably, bring such people into their organizations. The skills of institutional researchers to project populations, model the flow of specific groups, simulate program decisions, and develop cost-benefit models may be welcome planning and decision-support tools in development.

References

Council for the Advancement and Support of Education (CASE) and the National Association for College and University Business Officers (NACUBO). *Expenditure Guidelines and Definitions: An Analysis of Fund-Raising Expenditures.* Washington, D.C.: Council for the Advancement and Support of Education, 1986.

Dunn, J. A., Jr. (ed.). *Enhancing the Management of Fund Raising.* New Directions for Institutional Research, no. 51. San Francisco: Jossey-Bass, 1986.

Kotler, P. *Marketing for Nonprofit Organizations.* Englewood Cliffs, N.J.: Prentice-Hall, 1975.

Kotler, P. *Principles of Marketing.* Englewood Cliffs, N.J.: Prentice-Hall, 1983.

Paton, G. J. "Microeconomic Perspectives Applied to Development Planning and Management." In J. A. Dunn, Jr. (ed.), *Enhancing the Management of Fund Raising.* New Directions for Institutional Research, no. 51. San Francisco: Jossey-Bass, 1986.

Gerlinda S. Melchiori is deputy director of the Office of Administrative Services in the University of Michigan's Office of Development. She was project director for the University of Michigan's 1986 alumni census. She currently serves on the CASE Commission on Research.

Research on alumni can meet needs in program review,
curriculum planning, student assessment, resource allocation,
student services, and recruiting.

Applying Alumni Research to Decision Making

Gary O. Moden, A. Michael Williford

Alumni surveys have been used by colleges and universities for a number of years and for a variety of reasons. This chapter focuses on the use of alumni research in program review, curriculum planning, academic program planning, student assessment, resource allocation, and marketing and recruiting.

Pace (1979) identified ten landmark alumni studies reflecting the various ways alumni research can be used to assess the impact of an institution on its students. Many of these studies addressed similar issues—for example, job-related outcomes (occupational level, salary, job satisfaction) and educational outcomes (satisfaction with the educational experience, relationship of one's job to one's major program of study, the relevance of one's major to one's career goals) (p. 110). Alumni surveys, although not standardized across institutions, tend to pose similar questions and are probably the most widely used form of student assessment.

In general, graduates indicate in alumni surveys that they do indeed learn much while in college. They report developing critical-thinking abilities, acquiring knowledge and skills in specialized fields, and developing personal and social qualities and skills. They find professional, semiprofessional, or managerial jobs, earn respectable incomes, report satisfaction with their college experience, and would choose the same educational

G. S. Melchiori (ed.). *Alumni Research: Methods and Applications.*
New Directions for Institutional Research, no. 60. San Francisco: Jossey-Bass, Winter 1988.

path, given the chance to do it over again. They report that they like their jobs, that college experience is related to job and career, and that their educational experience broadened them in many ways (Pace, 1979).

The National Center for Higher Education Management Systems (1981) has suggested ways in which colleges and universities can use alumni research. First, alumni research provides information to academic planners about what happens to students after graduation, so that decisions can be made about the curriculum, faculty roles, and teaching methods. Second, alumni research can provide evidence of problems or needs in the curriculum, course content, and major requirements. Third, alumni research can provide guidance for the formation and offering of various student services. Fourth, alumni research provides information related to alumni and public relations. Fifth, alumni research, through all these other uses, can provide information to assist in resource allocation and institutional planning (p. 6).

Ohio University (Athens, Ohio) uses alumni research in most of these ways. The alumni research program has evolved over the last few years to provide different levels of the university with information for a variety of purposes that have strong implications for institutional researchers. Ohio University is a public residential university with an enrollment of approximately sixteen thousand students. It offers undergraduate, graduate, and professional degrees. The applications of alumni research outlined in this chapter are only examples of what can be done with alumni data. These applications can serve any institution, regardless of its size or type of control.

Background of Alumni Research at Ohio University

Alumni research is part of a commitment at Ohio University to assess the institution's impact on its students. An institutional-impact task force of faculty and staff was appointed in 1980 to meet with the director of institutional research and develop a coherent, systematic, and ongoing program to assess that impact. The primary goal of the assessment was for the university, in five to ten years, to be able to describe systematically what was happening in its life as an educational institution.

The task force spent about a year developing its program. This program considered such goals as providing students with the knowledge skills that are the essence of a solid liberal education and encouraging the development of a campus environment that would reflect a vital commitment to learning and provide a community life for students. To accommodate these basic goals, assessment was aimed at the broad impact of the collegiate experience, and not at specific knowledge and skills gained from a major field of study. The outcomes program provided a broad-based yet flexible set of measuring devices that enabled a breadth of information to be gathered. It was flexible in accepting new instruments as they became available and rejecting old ones as they became dated. The key issue in conducting assessment studies is whether the university can use the process of defining and examining its impact on students to enhance quality.

Earlier efforts had been successful to varying degrees in collecting information, because different academic colleges and departments used different instruments. While information collected from such surveys could be used within departments, the surveys did not allow for interdepartmental comparisons. To counter this problem, part of the design of the institutional-impact project included two separate instruments for alumni research. The first, a placement survey, was designed to collect information on graduates within one year of graduation. It collected information on employment status, acceptance into graduate or professional schools, and some limited information on employment satisfaction. The second, more detailed, survey was developed to study graduates after they had been away from the university for at least five years. The second questionnaire was divided into three major sections.

The first section asked about such traditional outcomes as type of job, employment status, salary, employment satisfaction, responsibilities, expectations, relevance of educational experience to employment, and problems in seeking employment. There was also a group of questions inquiring about various competencies needed for success. These questions asked respondents to evaluate fourteen different competencies in terms of both whether they were needed and the extent to which each had been developed at the university. They included the ability to think analytically, apply knowledge from the major field to new problems, acquire new skills and understanding, write well, communicate orally, evaluate and choose between alternative courses of action, and formulate creative and original ideas and solutions. Also included were the ability to convey meaning through artistic and creative expression, cope with complex moral and ethical issues, and place current problems in historical, cultural, and philosophical perspective. Finally, questions were asked concerning the need to use the political process, organize and supervise the work of others, use the computer as an analytical tool, and be sensitive to the feelings and perceptions of others.

The second section asked about programs of study and about satisfaction with undergraduate programs at Ohio University. Alumni were asked to rate their undergraduate major programs on relevance to career goals, academic advising, inspiration and encouragement, level of rigor and scholarship, interaction with faculty, quality of instruction, and career planning and placement associated with their majors.

"What if" questions were asked to determine whether alumni, if given a second chance, would make different choices. Would they change majors? Take more elective courses? Enroll in more general education? Take part in internships?

Questions were asked about additional coursework taken and degrees awarded since graduation. Information was collected on type of degree and institution that awarded the degree. Also, if alumni were anticipating additional academic work, they were asked to identify the degrees they would be seeking.

In the last four years of the study, each of the eight academic undergraduate colleges at the university participated in the development of the third section of the questionnaire, which contained college-specific questions. College-specific alumni data were needed for several reasons. The creation of a general, universitywide questionnaire precluded questions pertinent to specific academic disciplines. Since the institutional research office assumed the role of coordinating one large survey of alumni, in place of several college-administered surveys, the colleges lost their source of program-specific feedback. The coordinated survey, however, did provide information that had greater potential for use. Comparisons could be made among different units of the university. Trends of outcomes could be recorded from year to year. The addition of college-specific questions to the general questionnaire was well received at different levels of the university, since it not only provided the efficiency of conducting one survey instead of eight but also addressed program-specific needs for information.

Eight separate questionnaires were prepared. The first two sections of each one were identical, and the third was reserved for college-specific questions. Staff from the institutional research office worked with each college in designing these college-specific questions. The section for the college of arts and sciences included items on student services and non-major course requirements. The college of business administration developed items on teaching and advising and asked about participation in student organizations. The college of education asked thirty-seven questions about needed competencies. The college of engineering asked about academic programs, availability and quality of equipment, and nonmajor course requirements. The college of fine arts used items on employment opportunities and career preparation in the arts. The college of health and human services posed questions about continuing education after graduation, participation in professional organizations, use of microcomputers, and contacts with prospective students. The University College (general education) section asked questions about requirements, student services, and evaluation of the degree in general studies.

The entire populations of the classes were surveyed, to generate a response pool large enough to produce results specific to each academic college and department. This provided detailed reports for each academic unit that could be used for program evaluation and review. Had samples been used, many departments with few graduates would have had insufficient data.

General Applications of Alumni Research

Alumni research, along with the other outcomes measures, can be used for a variety of purposes, as suggested by Ewell (1983). Applications include academic program review and evaluation, retention, institutional planning, accreditation self-studies, and marketing and public relations. It is not surprising, then, that graduates' feedback in academic program review is gaining popularity on many campuses. For instance, alumni outcomes can be used for assessing the effectiveness of the general education program. At Ohio University, the dean of University College has been involved with the office of institutional research in identifying outcomes for general education through the use of the ACT College Outcomes Measures Program (COMP). Alumni study results complement COMP results by providing responses to questions about the program in general education, about what competencies are needed, and about the extent to which the program is achieving its purposes. The use of college-specific questions gave each of the academic colleges direct answers to curriculum-review questions that were related to courses in general education or major programs.

Information on study outcomes can be used in institutional planning and budget review, at several levels. For senior administrators, alumni information provides guidance in terms of the strengths and weaknesses of various aspects of the whole university. For example, information from alumni about the university's image affects the development and direction of public relations and recruiting. The university's planning and advisory council, which links budgeting and program planning, receives outcomes information for use in specific budget requests for new ventures. Departments and programs can use alumni research to document or support the need for new programs or changes in existing programs. Academic departments can use the success of their alumni to document support for additional faculty. Proponents of general education can provide feedback from alumni on the value of oral and written communications in today's job market to request additional funds for additional courses. Staff in career planning and placement can outline the importance of their mission, as viewed by alumni, to document the need for more programs and resources.

Application of Alumni Research
to Individual Academic Colleges

Reports of alumni research are presented to the Dean's Council on a regular basis, and information from these reports is incorporated into decision making. In addition, each college receives its own personalized report, designed to meet specific information needs. Staff from the institutional research office meet directly with the staff of the dean's office to review alumni research for particular colleges. This review includes executive summaries, as well as detailed analyses for academic departments within a college. Institutional research staff also attend departmental meetings and distribute results to all departments on the findings of research about their graduates. These meetings produce valuable feedback about the process and content of alumni research. For example, the institutional research staff has the opportunity to discuss changes in questions on the instrument, while departmental chairs have direct input in deciding what specific questions should be asked in the next survey.

The academic colleges have used the results of this data to develop a number of programs and evaluate different curricular options. For example, the college of arts and sciences was concerned about the perception of the college's numerous course requirements, which are in addition to general requirements. These include specific coursework in foreign languages, humanities, social sciences, and natural sciences. Responses from alumni led to the conclusion that this required coursework was important to the arts and sciences curriculum and was very relevant to graduates' careers. These findings eliminated the need for a faculty committee to review these questions, since the data provided feedback supporting current program requirements.

The college of arts and sciences also used the questionnaire results to develop a new awards program. Because information from the open-ended questions led to the conclusion that particular faculty had been extremely influential in graduates' personal development, the college instituted an awards program for faculty. Each year the college's Society of Alumni and Friends selects outstanding faculty to receive special recognition. Part of the information used for awards selection comes directly from the open-ended questions.

The college of business reviewed the alumni data in the aggregate for the college, and for each academic department within the college, to identify specific strengths and weaknesses of each academic unit. Alumni reported that they had not had enough contact with business executives while they were in their undergraduate degree programs. In response, the college developed the Executives on Campus Program, through which active business executives regularly visit the college and take an active role in undergraduate instruction.

Business graduates also reported a need to sharpen their writing skills. As a consequence, the college emphasized writing skills by changing courses to incorporate more written assignments, papers, and essays. In addition, multiple-choice tests were replaced, whenever possible, by essay examinations.

Data from alumni research were also used in job placement for graduates of the college of business. The college reviewed the types of positions and areas of employment of its graduates, and strengths of alumni were identified to assist currently strong programs. In areas where few alumni reported being employed, the college developed strategies to alleviate the shortage. This was accomplished by making contact with employers in these areas and encouraging the hiring of the college's graduates.

Information helpful in the recruitment process is used heavily by the college of communication. Because most communication majors are first-generation academics in the field, there is a lack of understanding about the career paths of communication graduates. For example, parents of entering students often ask, "What types of jobs can you get with a degree in communication?" Alumni research is used extensively in planning recruitment programs for new students and precollege orientation programs for parents and students that describe career paths, salaries, and examples of professional success of graduates of the college of communication.

Application of alumni research to the college of engineering assisted in planning. The college dean and its external advisory board were interested in developing a plan for the college for the 1990s. This process required an extensive environmental scan for the college, encompassing a review of both the internal and the external environments. The data collected by the institutional research office became an important part of this study by providing information about the strengths of its graduates in a volatile market for engineers.

External involvement of alumni concerning alumni research led directly to a change in the curriculum of the college of engineering. A member of Ohio University's national alumni board who was also a graduate of the college of engineering got involved with the college after reading an annual report on alumni generated by the institutional research office. On the basis of this report, the board member noted that while engineering graduates had been giving very high evaluations to the engineering program, they had also reported a lack of training in broad interpersonal communication in their undergraduate major. As a result of this finding, the board member met with the engineering dean to discuss incorporating more training in interpersonal communication into the engineering curriculum.

In the college of health and human services, alumni research is used for program review. The college uses research information to document the strengths and needs of its academic programs. This documentation is crucial since all university academic programs are reviewed every five years. Each department in the college develops profiles of its graduates to document their success, the quality of their preparation, and their ratings of the department's academic program.

Continuing education for alumni also relies on the use of alumni data. The college of health and human services collects information on its graduates' professional use of and need for microcomputers. Departmental faculty in each academic discipline then develop workshops to meet the reported needs of the alumni and offer them to alumni at appropriate times and locations.

The University College offers a baccalaureate degree in general studies, providing an opportunity for undergraduates to design their own education. The college is extremely interested in the careers of these graduates and uses alumni research to evaluate its program. In addition, data collected from alumni provide a valuable resource for prospective students about the types of career fields and life experiences they can expect after graduation.

The Ohio University program in general education was revised in the early 1980s, and its evaluation by alumni is being used as part of the criteria to measure its success. This use is especially revealing, because alumni who have experience of the previous program can be compared with alumni of the new program, and comparisons between the two programs can be used to evaluate the need for general education in today's job market.

Applying Alumni Research to Funding and External Evaluation

The funding of academic programs can be enhanced by alumni research documenting the success of graduates. In the past four years, the Ohio state legislature has established enrichment grants at colleges and universities judged to have programs of high quality. Outcomes information on alumni has been used by four academic departments at Ohio University in their proposals for recent awards. The honors tutorial college and the departments of journalism, telecommunications, and visual communications all have used such information to document the success of their students in this statewide academic competition for enrichment grants. A total of about $650,000 has been awarded to these departments.

Alumni outcomes can also be used for accreditation review and self-study. The university reported traditional information on alumni, such as salary, job placement, type of occupation, and continuing education, to demonstrate follow-up of students and to document students' success to accrediting agencies. College-specific questions are used for the same purpose. For example, the college of education asked thirty-seven questions related to aspects of education instruction that have been used in accreditation reviews by the National Center for Accreditation of Teacher Education.

Alumni information is of great value in marketing, recruiting, career planning and placement, and public relations. For example, alumni research provides evidence of students' success that can be documented for use in admissions publications. The collection of alumni information demonstrates an interest in keeping track of students after graduation. Outcomes information is used by enrollment planners to show characteristics of program completers, so that those characteristics can be sought in prospective students. Outcomes information gives staff in career planning and placement realistic information about job trends and career paths of graduates, which can be communicated to current students who are about to begin the job-search process. Ohio University's National Alumni Board also receives a briefing each year on some aspect of the assessment system from the institutional research office. In addition, the director of alumni relations forwards assessment reports to all members of the national alumni board.

Implications for Institutional Researchers

The purpose of this chapter has been to provide an example of the variety of uses of alumni research on a single campus. Maximum use of alumni information should be a goal of all institutional researchers who are involved with alumni research. Some helpful strategies by which institutional researchers can play a pivotal role in the development and maintenance of useful alumni research programs are apparent from this chapter.

Alumni research information needs to be presented at different administrative levels within an institution. Different levels have different uses for the information they receive, and they may require different forms and different levels of detail. For example, the admissions office may seek evidence of the success of students, while academic divisions may use the information for program review. Different levels of presentation require different formats. Certain departments may not require extensive summaries of findings; they may be interested only in the results for their own graduates. Comparative information may be needed at the senior administrative level, although it may not be appropriate at other levels.

Alumni research collects both general and program-specific information, often simultaneously. The key to using these data successfully is flexibility in meeting and melding a variety of information needs. Through careful coordination with many campus constituencies, this information can be applied to a variety of programs.

References

Ewell, P. T. *Student Outcomes Questionnaires: An Implementation Handbook.* Boulder, Colo.: National Center for Higher Education Management Systems, 1983.

National Center for Higher Education Management Systems. *A Demonstration Grant: Assistance to Seven Public Institutions in Improving Their Use of Student Outcomes Information in Decision Making and Academic Program Planning.* Boulder, Colo.: National Center for Higher Education Management Systems, 1981.

Pace, C. *Measuring Outcomes of College: Fifty Years of Findings and Recommendations for the Future.* San Francisco: Jossey-Bass, 1979.

Gary O. Moden is director of the Office of Institutional Research and assistant professor in the School of Applied Behavior Sciences and Educational Leadership at Ohio University.

A. Michael Williford is assistant director of the Office of Institutional Research at Ohio University.

*Alumni are the institution's extended family. What do
you have to know and do to keep the relationships warm,
knowledgeable, and mutually supportive?*

The Future Agenda
for Alumni Research

John A. Dunn, Jr.

Collection of information on alumni is nothing new, but alumni research
is growing rapidly. For years, colleges and universities have kept track of
their graduates, asking them for political and financial support and for
help in recruiting students. For these purposes, the institutions needed
some historical information, such as year of graduation, degree received,
and involvement in sports or fraternities, if any; some personal information, including nickname, marital status, married name (if different),
names of children who might be prospects; and some current information, such as address, number, telephone, and job title. Almost every
college makes an attempt to capture and retain this information, at least
on alumni and on those whom it feels are most important. Research on
this sketchy information was usually limited to such things as counts of
alumni by degree or by state or congressional district. More sophisticated
alumni research efforts usually had to do with fundraising and were
therefore focused on indicators of wealth, current income, and areas of
interest, as indicated by prior gifts.

The fact that the Association for Institutional Research thought that
the topic of alumni research merited a *New Directions for Institutional
Research* volume is testimony to the fact this this simple picture is beginning to change. One shift has to do with the volume of data and the

G. S. Melchiori (ed.). *Alumni Research: Methods and Applications.*
New Directions for Institutional Research, no. 60. San Francisco: Jossey-Bass, Winter 1988.

analytic sophistication needed to support modern development efforts. Public universities with enormous alumni populations began serious fundraising efforts during the last decade. Public and private institutions, both large and small, sought alumni support in more aggressive ways and needed additional information to focus those efforts. With better information on a large fraction of the alumni population, institutions have been able to ask and answer far more sophisticated questions in understanding alumni attitudes and identifying prospective donors. The data-management skills needed to create and feed these alumni databases, and the analytical and computer skills needed to extract desired information, are often beyond the traditional capabilities of personnel in alumni relations and development. Similar changes are taking place in smaller liberal arts and community colleges. Their development efforts, previously limited and personalized, now require extensive information as the institutions attempt to solicit broader constituencies.

Yet another change is that offices in addition to development are now interested in alumni data. As academic administrators assess their curricula, they want to sample graduates' retrospective evaluations and track their careers. Staff in career guidance use alumni to introduce students to possible occupations and to place them in internships and summer jobs. Admissions officers count heavily on alumni to recruit and interview prospective students.

This chapter is focused on the future agenda for alumni research and has two main sections. The first is a plea for the standardization of terminology in the field. It includes a first effort at a taxonomy and at a strategy for achieving the standardization. The chapter then moves directly to a listing of research questions in various areas of alumni giving, alumni activities, and support for alumni.

A Terminology for Thinking About Alumni Research

Although individual institutions and small consortia may do valuable research on their own alumni, broader and more useful comparative and statistical studies must await the development of both a comprehensive and precise taxonomy and a proved and practical set of survey instruments. In their absence, researchers cannot be sure that their samples, their procedures, or their results are comparable.

In recent work on standardized gift reporting and on the classification of development expenditures, the Council for the Advancement and Support of Education (CASE) (1981), together with the National Association for College and University Business Officers (CASE/NACUBO, 1986), has demonstrated a successful procedure for attacking such major definitional projects. In each case, national professional organizations defined the nature, intent, and scope of the project, and gave it a high priority for committees and staffs. They then sought and obtained outside support (in the CASE/NACUBO projects, from the Exxon Education Foundation and the Lilly Endowment). A committee of leading figures in the field developed initial drafts of the definitions and guidelines. These were shared with a selected sample of interested institutions that used them on a trial basis, reported any difficulties, and suggested modifications. Finally, after repeated revisions, the definitions were adopted officially by the professional organizations and made part of standard practice in the field.

In developing a taxonomy, it can be helpful to have an overall organizing concept. Larry Litten of the Council on the Financing of Higher Education suggested in a recent personal conversation that the alumni of an institution are best thought of as its extended family. That analogy is useful in thinking about the kinds of information we might like to have. What would present and prospective family members like to know? What would sociologists looking at family structure and relationships want to know? What would parents want to know? We are primarily interested in the current relationships between the alumni family and the institution, recognizing that those relationships will vary on the basis of characteristics of the alumnus or the alumnae and of his or her experience at the institution.

Conceptual Taxonomy, Part A: Current information on alumni and on their current relationship to the institution. The first level of categories in this area would include the kinds of data listed below.

Current Demographics. How can the family be characterized? What is the distribution of members on age, socioeconomic and occupational status, attitudes, values? On these measures, how do the family data compare to those for the nation or the region, or for similar institutions? What are the career paths of various family members, and how do they relate to the educational programs? How do members feel about belonging to the family? What is the social and occupational role of alumni status? (In this area lies the range of data of interest in estimation of wealth.)

Attitudes Toward the Institution. How do family members feel about the institution? What is their degree of loyalty? How informed are they about current institutional activities and priorities, and how supportive are they in these areas? What feedback can they give to the institution on specific programs? (In this area lies the whole set of questions regarding alumni information useful in the assessment of institutions and programs, and in estimating inclination to give.)

Involvement with the Institution. How are family members involved with the ongoing life of the institution—admissions, placement, counseling, donating, and involvement in school activities? (In this area lie the research topics suggested later with regard to the patterns of alumni giving.)

Institutional Support for Alumni. How does the institution support the family? Through publications, career counseling, activities and organizations, continuing education opportunities? (In this area lie the research topics suggested later with respect to alumni offices.)

Conceptual Taxonomy, Part B: Original characteristics of the alumni and of their experience at the institution. While the questions already listed will be pertinent to the broad range of colleges and universities in this country, responses will vary on the basis of the characteristics of institutions and graduates' enrollment experiences.

Initial Demographics. How does the experience of alumni differ because of gender, ethnic group, or other characteristics? What special things do we want to know about each group?

School or Program Involved? Alumni of a school's undergraduate programs are likely to differ in important ways (primary loyalty, socioeconomic background, earning power) from those of its graduate or professional programs. There may also be significant differences at the undergraduate level between liberal arts alumni and those from engineering, nursing, or occupationally related programs.

Duration and Character of Association. In admissions research, it is common to visualize a funnel that is wide at one end, to include all potential students, and that then narrows through the various stages of actual inquiries, completed applications, accepted students, and matriculants. For alumni research, we need to distinguish between all those who ever enrolled, those with significant attendance (one or more years), and those who completed one or more programs. The early dropouts will hardly ever be loyal alumni, but it is gratifying to find the occasional alumnus who, despite never having completed the degree, is a loyal fan and a substantial contributor. It would also be useful to know students' initial educational aspirations, if such data could be identified. For community colleges, for instance, it would be important to distinguish among those who wanted only individual courses, those who were enrolling to see whether they liked college, those who planned to complete only the associate degree, and those who wanted associate-level preparation for transfer.

Time Since Enrollment. Connolly and Blanchette (1986) found that the interest among alumni in increasing their annual donations to one institution declined steadily with time since graduation. Is this pattern duplicated elsewhere and in other areas of alumni interest and involvement? Are there subtle but important shifts in areas of alumni interest over time? For instance, at what time, and for what groups of alumni, does interest among attendees at reunions shift from remembering what it was like when they were there to discussing what alumni are doing now? At what point has enough time intervened for the institution to be able to convey to alumni how it has changed since their graduation?

Uses of Standardized Instruments. As terminology and standard questions are developed, and as a number of institutions begin to report their data in these categories, it would be particularly useful for researchers to carry out systematic surveys of what is now known in each of these areas, both in published studies and in internal institutional documents. These surveys could be the basis of identifying interesting and useful areas for further work.

In addition to providing important data for fundraising plans, program assessment, and other operational matters, the standard questions already noted could provide interesting and instructive information in a number of ways:

- In characterizing a particular institution in comparison with peer or rival institutions
- In monitoring changes over time in that institution's profile of alumni and donor attitudes (a college or university might, for instance, wish to take before-and-after readings with respect to a capital campaign, a major consciousness-raising effort, a change in president, a winning football or basketball season, or an announced change in mission)
- In characterizing sectors of postsecondary education, state systems, and so on
- In linking alumni research with information gathered by national professional organizations searching for new insights into relationships among schooling, attitudes, and career practice and patterns
- In pursuing large-scale sociological research comparing graduates of higher education with other social groups (the national census, national labor statistics, and tax data are only a few types of large bodies of information that could add macro dimensions to alumni research).

Suggested Areas for Future Alumni Research

A clear and comprehensive taxonomy and tested survey questions will significantly facilitate alumni research and enhance its reliability and comparability among institutions. The development of these basics, however, will require a number of years. Meanwhile, institutions need information, and researchers do have an agenda of topics on which to concentrate.

Donor research is the longest-lived, most widespread and most intense area of alumni research. Because of the stakes involved, much of this work is already highly sophisticated. This chapter concentrates on questions on which further effort seems likely to be well rewarded.

Measurement of Wealth. It is important to be able to measure fundraising performance against fundraising potential, to judge the effectiveness of current efforts and evaluate the likely benefits of further investment. Intuitively, it seems clear that institutions vary widely in their potential. Pickett (1982) made a vital first attempt at measuring fundraising potential as a function of the resources available to the institution (number of alumni, and regional characteristics such as family income, manufacturing value-added, and foundation grant activity) and resource-related characteristics of the institution (age of the institution, enrollment, endowment value, cost of attendance, and so on).

A different approach was taken by Paton (1986), who pointed out that giving by alumni, as well as by nonalumni, can also be thought of as a function of wealth and inclination. Alumni can be queried directly about the inclination to support the alma mater (a standard practice of institutions planning development campaigns). Likelihood of giving can also be estimated from responses to alumni surveys (Connolly and Blanchette, 1986). Of course, colleges can influence the inclination to give by the way they treat donors over time, by the merit of their appeals, and by the artistry of their presentations. What is not under institutional control (except, to some degree, through the admissions process) is alumni wealth. Estimating fundraising potential comes down to estimating wealth. Alumni researchers do this in individual cases, for major prospects. What statistical work can be done to view the alumni population as a whole? Current income can be reasonably estimated from an occupation or a job title. Accumulated or inherited wealth might be estimated statistically from analysis of housing prices, lot sizes, housing turnover rates, and other characteristics of the census districts in which alumni reside, as well as from analyses of social registers, list of members of prestigious clubs and boards, and so on. While such statistical approaches are time-consuming and limited in their analytical power, they may provide useful estimates of wealth, and therefore of institutional fundraising potential.

Model Development in Alumni Giving. Fundraising is both an art and a science. There is high art in matching an institution's major needs with the interests of major prospective donors, in helping the donor to see the need and take pride in helping in a substantial way. Nevertheless, identifying prospective major donors, and soliciting the great mass of modest and small donors in the most effective ways, also constitute no small science.

Many modeling approaches can be taken to this goal-setting and managerial task. In setting the targets for capital campaigns, it is important to develop a gift table showing the number of gifts at each size level that will be needed to reach the overall target (see Bennett and Hays, 1986). This analysis involves the study of past giving patterns, the analysis of the prospective donor pool, and an evaluative matching of projects and prospects. Once the campaign is under way, constant measurement of progress against the gift table can help refocus the tactics needed to ensure success.

A second application involves the use of spreadsheet models of the patterns of alumni giving, by gift size and year of graduation, to predict and set targets for annual campaigns (see Dunn, 1985). Finally, many institutions use a sophisticated prospect-tracking process to manage their fundraising activities. Fundraisers are assigned sets of prospects with already-rated potential and are then monitored on activity indicators (number of contacts, number of solicitations, number of closes) and on success factors (dollars solicited in relation to potential, dollars contributed in relation to potential and to amount solicited).

Each of these techniques is likely to be more widely used and further developed as better information becomes available. Target setting, for instance, can be adapted to shifting patterns of institutional fundraising, focused on reunion giving or on major solicitations or on mail and phone campaigns. Its accuracy can be improved as better information on alumni becomes available and as records of prior-year activities are kept and analyzed with these questions in mind.

Other Areas of Alumni Fundraising Research. Other questions of interest include the following, in rough order of priority.

1. *Planned giving:* This is an area of rapidly growing importance for institutions seeking very sizable gifts. Who gives planned gifts? There are various mechanisms for doing so. Which works best with what kinds of donors? What measure of potential is useful in this area? Is there some actuarial basis for calibrating overall potential and performance in this area?

2. *Donors:* It has often been said that the best prospects for new gifts are people who have already given, perhaps even those who have already given in the current campaign. What can be discovered about attitudes and involvements before and after giving? How are donors acknowledged? What stewardship functions are carried on in institutions with successful programs, and do they appear to make a difference with respect to subsequent giving?

3. *Alumni questionnaires:* Earlier chapters in this book address this question, but it remains a fertile field for additional approaches (see also Connolly and Blanchette, 1986).

4. *Pledge fulfillment:* What default rates are experienced? From what kinds of donors? When? On what kinds of pledges? Under what conditions?

5. *Multiple-degree holders:* When individuals hold two or more degrees from an institution, what, if anything, can be said about their overall giving in comparison to single-degree holders, and about their support for one school versus another?

6. *Nongivers:* Who declines to give when asked or gives far less than the potential or solicited amount? What can we tell about these alumni?

7. *Nonrespondents to questionnaires:* Who drops out? What can we tell about them?

Thus far, we have focused exclusively on alumni research related to fundraising. Now we move on to research concerning other kinds of alumni activities, offices, and organizations.

Involvement in Alumni Activities. What activities are alumni involved in, formally and informally? What fraction of the alumni population is so involved, and which alumni participate?

What kinds of influence do alumni exert? What formal relationships do they hold to the institution (election of trustees, or requirements that some fraction of the board be made up of alumni)?

How are alumni organized? What is the relationship of organization type to the kinds of activities supported, alumni attitudes, and so on? To what extent are the formal alumni organizations representative of (and captive of) subgroups of alumni, such as those who are local, who are ex-athletes, who are of a particular age group, or who are fraternity-related?

What are the roles of alumni councils, or similar organizations, with respect to alumni affairs, institutional activities, and policies? Do these relationships vary by type of organization? In what ways, if at all, does the form of an alumni organization affect the influence that alumni can have?

Alumni Office Personnel, Missions, and Budgets. Who works in alumni offices? What are the typical staffing patterns in terms of exempt and nonexempt, part-time, and full time personnel? What backgrounds do they have? What proportion of them are graduates of the institution? What are their career paths? What training do they have? Development personnel have the reputation of moving frequently, with consequent high training costs and disruption of donor relations. Carbone (1987), for instance, found that 55 percent of fundraisers had been in their current positions two years or less. Thomas (1987) found that turnover in alumni relations offices ran at 13.9 percent annually, high in comparison to other kinds of careers but low in relation to development (19.5 percent) and public relations offices (18.2 percent). Does this turnover vary by type of institution, or by level? Does the chief alumni officer tend to stay on each year with a new cadre of juniors?

What are the missions or goals that are articulated for alumni offices and their activities? How many such offices even have statements of goals or objectives, and in what kinds of institutions is one apt to find specifically articulated goals? How do these goals differ by type of institution?

How does the alumni office relate to other activities (development, public relations) of the institution? How does it relate to other campus offices (institutional research, academic departments, the registrar)? To whom does the director report? What is the relationship of publications programs among the alumni office, the public relations office, the publications office, and the development office? Do the job descriptions of personnel in the alumni office include any other functions? Do the job descriptions of other development personnel include any functions of alumni relations? How are these coordinated? How does compensation for personnel in the alumni office compare to that for other development personnel?

What effort is put into alumni activities by different kinds of institutions? Is effort best gauged by staffing levels, by proportions of educational and general budgets dedicated to this activity, by size of the alumni body, or by other measures? How can one relate this effort to some measure of attainment of goals or objectives, or to other measures of effectiveness? What measures of cost-effectiveness can one construct in this area?

What do budgets for alumni relations look like? Of what elements are they composed? What proportion of the budget goes for each type of expenditure (staffing, travel, publications)?

To what extent, and in what ways, do the alumni offices and their organizations generate revenue that helps sustain their activities? What happens to these revenues? How are they budgeted for?

To what extent, and for what kinds of functions, are consultants used? Can their use be related to types of goals or types of institutions? How does one measure their effectiveness?

Are there economies of scale in alumni relations? What is the relationship of staffing in alumni and development offices in relationship to alumni populations? Does this differ by type of institution?

Further Alumni Research Concerning Assessment. Another major area for growth in alumni research will be assessment of educational programs (see Ewell, 1985). The directions of this kind of growth would seem to be the development of more sophisticated survey instruments, much broader sampling of judgments on educational experiences, and more systematic career tracking.

Further Development Research. A number of research questions related to fundraising are only tangentially related to alumni research. Nevertheless, they seem to deserve a place in a listing of promising future projects. Fundraising professionals will have a fairly good intuitive sense of the answers to many of these questions, but careful examination may produce surprising and helpful results and cause a reallocation of development resources.

What is the cost differential and the outcome differential between mail, phone, and personal solicitations? Do any differences in these results depend on time since graduation? on degree held? on type of institution? To what extent does soliciting for a specific goal, versus for the institution in general, influence the amounts raised? To what extent do frequency of contact and mix of approaches influence the amount and frequency of alumni giving?

Can the impact of certain activities (alumni and donor events, recognition levels, giving clubs, football get-togethers, deans' parties, personalized acknowledgments, and the like) be empirically assessed? If so, where is the point of diminishing returns?

Much of the currently evolving learning focuses on the programmatic components, policies, and ethics of fundraising, but little in-depth research has emerged on the actual qualifications of professionals in the field. What kinds of matches should one look for between the personality and background of the development officer and the type of fundraising and institution involved?

What are the relevant strengths of centralized, decentralized, and mixed organizational structures for fundraising? What empirical evidence (money raised, cost, staff resources used) supports experience-based beliefs in this area, or arguments for change? Are institution-specific cost-benefit models (which typically cannot be compared easily with those of other institutions) the only support information available in arguing for one structure over another?

Many institutions have only recently developed comprehensive fundraising offices, and their activities have therefore received above-average budgetary allocation and consideration. We are rapidly approaching the point where more and more senior decision makers, who by now realize that these functions are here to stay, will want to assess efficiency and effectiveness. Major efforts are already under way to develop realistic methods of evaluating cost-effectiveness and program efficiency, but several factors complicate the task of institutional comparison. These include questions of whether an institution is engaged in a major campaign, to what extent the development functions are at a mature level or still in the developmental phase, to what extent senior executives and trustees are engaged in the fundraising effort, whether the cost-collecting process assesses the work contributed by all personnel (deans, faculty, lawyers), differences between institutions in characteristics of alumni, and such basic distinctions as public versus private, institutional degree levels and size, and the like.

Alumni are the institution's extended family. As we awaken to that fact, we find we need to know and do a great deal more than we have in the past to keep the relationships warm, knowledgeable, and mutually supportive. Alumni research is not a new field, but it should expand rapidly in sophistication and in importance to institutions of higher learning in the next decade.

References

Bennett, R. L., and Hays, J. C. "Setting Targets for a Successful Capital Campaign." In J. A. Dunn, Jr. (ed.), *Enhancing the Management of Fund Raising.* New Directions for Institutional Research, no. 51. San Francisco: Jossey-Bass, 1986.

Carbone, R. F. *Fund Raisers of Academe*. College Park, Md.: Clearinghouse for Research on Fund Raising, University of Maryland, 1987.

Connolly, M. S., and Blanchette, R. "Understanding and Predicting Alumni Giving Behavior." In J. A. Dunn, Jr. (ed.), *Enhancing the Management of Fund Raising*. New Directions for Institutional Research, no. 51. San Francisco: Jossey-Bass, 1986.

Council for the Advancement and Support of Education (CASE) and the National Association for College and University Business Officers (NACUBO). *Gift Reporting Standards and Management Reports for Educational Institutions*. Washington, D.C.: Council for the Advancement and Support of Education, 1981.

Council for the Advancement and Support of Education (CASE) and the National Association for College and University Business Officers (NACUBO). *Expenditure Guidelines and Definitions: An Analysis of Fund-Raising Expenditures*. Washington, D.C.: Council for the Advancement and Support of Education, 1986.

Dunn, J. A., Jr. "Modeling Alumni/ae Annual Fund Participation: A Partial Success at a Liberal Arts College." Paper presented at the annual conference of the North East Association for Institutional Research, Hartford, Conn., 1985.

Ewell, P. T. (ed.). *Assessing Educational Outcomes*. New Directions for Institutional Research, no. 47. San Francisco: Jossey-Bass, 1985.

Paton, G. J. "Microeconomic Perspectives Applied to Development Planning and Management." In J. A. Dunn, Jr. (ed.), *Enhancing the Management of Fund Raising*. New Directions for Institutional Research, no. 51. San Francisco: Jossey-Bass, 1986.

Pickett, W. L. "What Determines Fund-Raising Effectiveness?" *CASE Currents*, January 1982, pp. 22–25.

Thomas, E. G. "Flight Records." *CASE Currents*, October 1987, pp. 6–11.

John A. Dunn, Jr., is vice-president for planning at Tufts University and has worked with the development staffs at Tufts and at Wesleyan University in planning their fundraising activities.

Alumni research does not yet have its own body of literature and resources. Therefore, further readings were selected from various related areas, such as fundraising, marketing, survey research, and other resource books.

Selected References for Alumni Research

Gerlinda S. Melchiori

General

Carbone, R. F. *An Agenda for Research on Fund Raising.* College Park, Md.: Clearinghouse for Research on Fund Raising, University of Maryland, 1986.

This pamphlet describes the many unresearched areas in fundraising. Alumni research appears in several sections.

Dunn, J. A., Jr. (ed.). *Enhancing the Management of Fund Raising.* New Directions for Institutional Research, no. 51. San Francisco: Jossey-Bass, 1986.

This sourcebook has several articles on fundraising research in general, and donor research in particular.

Ewell, P. T. (ed.). *Assessing Educational Outcomes.* New Directions for Institutional Research, no. 47. San Francisco: Jossey-Bass, 1985.

This sourcebook deals with graduates, not as providers of funds and networks but as consumers of higher education. The volume concentrates on analyzing the impact higher education has had on students for institutional and curricular review.

G. S. Melchiori (ed.). *Alumni Research: Methods and Applications.*
New Directions for Institutional Research, no. 60. San Francisco: Jossey-Bass, Winter 1988.

Kotler, P. *Marketing for Nonprofit Organizations*. Englewood Cliffs, N.J.: Prentice-Hall, 1975.

This still is a very good book to acquaint researchers with the principles of marketing, especially the process of segmenting markets in nonprofit organizations.

Melchiori, G. S. "Ranking Achievement." *CASE Currents*, 1988, *14* (7).

This article focuses on using alumni data to develop an in-house prospect ranking system.

Pace, C. *Measuring Outcomes of College: Fifty Years of Findings and Recommendations for the Future*. San Francisco: Jossey-Bass, 1979.

This book is a classic and a good introduction to research on student outcomes.

Managing Information on Alumni

The following resources are among those most useful in planning systems and maintaining current information on alumni. The inclusion here of specific services should not be construed as an endorsement of them; they are listed for informational purposes only.

Periodicals and Publications

Blakely, B. E. *Alumni Administration at State Colleges and Universities*. Washington, D.C.: Council for the Advancement and Support of Education, 1979.

CASE Currents, 1986, *12* (8), entire issue.

This issue addresses the uses of computerized operations in development work. Among its topics are the use of online databases in donor-prospect research, computerized integration of information, and getting survey information onto computers.

Fund Raising Management, 1987, *18* (5), entire issue.

This issue focuses on the computerization of development activities. Articles evaluate software designed to manage the records of nonprofit organizations, techniques for computerizing a small development office, and design of information systems.

Gorman, B. *Finding Lost Alumni: Tracing Methods Used by 19 Institutions*. Washington, D.C.: Council for the Advancement and Support of Education, 1981.

"A Program Takes Charge of Records Management." *Modern Office Technology,* March 1988, pp. 70–72, 74, 78.

This article reports on a large-scale document-management system developed by Southern California Edison. Although the system is non-academic in orientation and far larger than any academic systems, the concepts that control it are easily transferable.

Online Information Services

There are many online services; all require a computer and a modem to access. Those listed below are the ones most often used to retrieve information on alumni and their businesses.

DIALOG Information Services, 3460 Hillview Ave., Palo Alto, CA 94304, (808) 334-2564

DIALOG is the largest information service, with approximately three hundred databases, and provides more academically oriented databases than any other service. The *Who's Who* database is useful in alumni records management, as are the several full-text electronic versions of major newspapers.

Dow Jones News Retrieval, Dow Jones & Co., Inc., P.O. Box 300, Princeton, NJ 08540, (800) 257-5114

Some of Dow Jones's databases duplicate those offered by DIALOG. However, the full-text electronic versions of the *Wall Street Journal* and the *Washington Post* offered here are invaluable.

Dun & Bradstreet Credit Services, One Diamond Hill Rd., Murray Hill, NJ 07974, (800) 472-4748

Dun & Bradstreet Credit Services provides financial information on public and private companies. It also includes biographical sketches of officers and directors and often lists their academic credentials.

VU/TEXT Information Services, 1211 Chestnut St., Philadelphia, PA 19107, (800) 258-8080

VU/TEXT offers approximately thirty full-text electronic newspapers, as well as magazines, newswires, and some business-oriented databases. Its databases can be searched online. It also offers automatic searches for specific information, such as alumni obituaries.

Regional and National Credit Bureaus

These bureaus offer online tracing of address changes. A social security number is required. Two credit bureau services with national coverage are TRW and TransUnion. Check local credit bureaus for available services and costs.

Telephone Matching Services

Clients supply current names and addresses, and the service searches for telephone numbers that correspond. This service is a valuable one for institutions planning telethons or telephone surveys.

Telematch, a service of Army Times Telephone Marketing Company, 475 School St., S.W., Washington, DC 20024, (202) 554-7782

Telematch requires that names and addresses be submitted on magnetic computer tape.

Telephone Lookup Service, 937 New Rodgers Rd., Levittown, PA 19056, (215) 752-8206

This service accepts hard-copy names and addresses.

National Change-of-Address (NCOA) Vendors

These vendors maintain the U.S. Postal Service's NCOA database. Unlike the Postal Service, which keeps change-of-address information for only six months, the vendors keep the information for as long as two years.

AT&T American Transtech, 8000 Bay Meadows Way, Jacksonville, FL 32216, (904) 636-2027

Credit Bureau Marketing, 8440 Westpark, Houston, TX 77063, (713) 954-6400

Tracing Services

CPC Associates, 33 Rock Hill Rd., Bala-Cynwyd, PA 19004, (215) 667-1780

This firm uses multiple sources to locate new addresses.

Wogan & Associates, 3055 W. 111th St., Suite 3 North, Chicago, IL 60655, (312) 779-3700

Wogan & Associates uses nongovernment databases to locate new addresses. Social security numbers are required.

Surveying Your Alumni

Council for the Advancement and Support of Education. *Surveying Your Alumni*. Washington, D.C.: Council for the Advancement and Support of Education, 1983.

This resource manual includes five articles on alumni survey techniques, both mail and telephone, as well as samples of survey questionnaires from twenty-two institutions.

Ewell, P. T. *Student Outcomes Questionnaires: An Implementation Handbook.* Boulder, Colo.: National Center for Higher Education Management Systems, 1983.

This is one of the best sources available for methods of conducting research on student outcomes.

Miller, A. F. (ed.). *A College in Dispersion.* Boulder, Colo.: Westview Press, 1976.

This book is the report of the information collected by Bryn Mawr's 1970 alumni census. The introduction outlines the survey process, and the content details the wealth of data that can be compiled from a comprehensive analysis of survey responses.

National Center for Higher Education Management Systems. *A Demonstration Grant: Assistance to Seven Public Institutions in Improving Their Use of Student Outcomes Information in Decision Making and Academic Program Planning.* Boulder, Colo.: National Center for Higher Education Management Systems, 1981.

Alumni Data Analysis

While many general statistical books are available, the following references were particularly helpful in specific statistical procedures.

Andrews, F. M., Morgan, J. N., Sonquist, J. A., and Klem, L. *Multiple Classification Analysis.* (2nd ed.) Ann Arbor, Mich.: Institute for Social Research, 1973.

Sonquist, J. A., Baker, E. L., and Morgan, J. N. *Searching for Structure.* (Rev. ed.) Ann Arbor, Mich.: Institute for Social Research, 1973.

All of the statistical procedures discussed in this sourcebook are part of the OSIRIS—IV Data Management and Statistical Analysis software package, an alternative to SAS and SPSS. This comprehensive software package currently has nine higher education installations (including Harvard, UCLA, the Universities of Alberta and British Columbia), twenty-one commercial installations (including five IBM installations, Donnelley Marketing Information Systems, and Social Surveys [Gallup Poll] Limited, three U.S. Government installations (including the Internal Revenue Service and the Census Bureau as a test site for new systems), and is accessible to numerous educational institutions through the MERIT and

MTS networks. OSIRIS-IV is available on a license basis through the Survey Research Center, Institute for Social Research, The University of Michigan, P.O. Box 1248, Ann Arbor, MI 48106.

SEARCH is unique to OSIRIS-IV and is not available in SAS or SPSS. Other alternatives, although limited in capabilities, are CART, from Statistical Software (Berkeley, California), and SI-CHAID, from Statistical Innovations (Belmont, Massachusetts).

Gerlinda S. Melchiori is deputy director of the Office of Administrative Services in the University of Michigan's Office of Development. She was project director of the University of Michigan's 1986 alumni census. She currently serves on the CASE Commission on Research.

Index

A

Accreditation, and alumni outcomes, 74
Alberta, University of, data analysis at, 93
Alumni: associate, 9; cumulative impact of, 52-53; defining, 7-9; degree, 7-8; involvement in activities for, 84; nondegree, 8-9; projecting growth of, 51-53; services of, 9-10; subtracting, 52
Alumni office, research needed on, 84-85
Alumni research: analysis of evolution of, 5-11; background on, 5-6; barriers to, 6-7, 54; conclusion on, 11; on current information, 79-80; data analysis for, 39-50; decision-making applications of, 67-76; defining, 9-10; fundraising applications of, 51-65, 83-84; future agenda for, 77-87; growth of, 77-78; information systems for, 13-23; instruments for, 29-30, 69-70, 81; on measurement of wealth, 81-82; on models of giving, 82-83; on original characteristics and experiences, 80; resources on, 89-94; surveys for, 25-38; taxonomy for, 78-81; uses of, 1, 10-11, 68
American College Testing (ACT) Program, 71
Andrews, F. M., 45, 49, 93
Aristotle, 1
Army Times Telephone Marketing Company, 92
Arts and sciences colleges, alumni research for, 70, 72
Assessment research: and alumni research, 9; future needs in, 85
Association for Institutional Research (AIR), 1, 7, 77
AT&T American Transtech, 92

B

Baker, E. L., 46, 49, 93
Bennett, R. L., 82, 86
Binary splits: for data analysis, 46-48; fundraising applications of, 59
Blakely, B. E., 90
Blanchette, R., 80, 82, 83, 87
British Columbia, University of, data analysis at, 93
Bryn Mawr, alumni survey by, 29, 31, 34, 36, 93
Business colleges, alumni research for, 70, 72-73

C

California at Los Angeles, University of (UCLA), data analysis at, 93
Calvin College, alumni survey by, 35
Carbone, R. F., 27, 39, 84, 87, 89
Centers for Philanthropic Research, 2, 7
Change of address, vendors for, 21, 92
Cohen, J., 45, 49
Cohen, P., 45, 49
College Outcomes Measures Program (COMP), 71
Communication colleges, alumni research for, 73
Community colleges: alumni defining by, 8-9; alumni research used by, 10
Confidentiality, of survey responses, 30
Connolly, M. S., 80, 82, 83, 87
Costs: of fundraising, 62; of surveys, 37-38
Council for the Advancement and Support of Education (CASE), 1-2, 7, 8, 14, 26-27, 34, 38, 62, 65, 78-79, 87, 90, 92

Council on the Financing of Higher Education, 79
CPC Associates, 92
Credit Bureau Marketing, 92
Credit bureaus, and information systems, 91, 92

D

Data analysis: aspects of, 39-50; audience for, 48-49; data fields for, 41; and data preparation, 39-43; data set for, 43; and dissemination, 48-49; inputting for, 40-41; organizing, 43-48; profiles for, 44; ranking for, 44-48; recoding for, 41-42; resources on, 93; sampling for, 42; segmentation for, 42, 43-44; verification for, 41
Decision making: alumni research applications for, 67-76; background on, 67-68; dissemination of findings for, 71-74; for funding and external evaluation, 74-75; and institutional-impact task force, 68-71; and institutional research implications, 75
Development research, future needs in, 85-86
DIALOG Information Services, 91
Dissemination: and data analysis, 48-49; for decision making, 71-74
Doke, L., 8, 11
Donnelley Marketing Information Systems, data analysis at, 93
Dow Jones News Retrieval, 91
Duke University: census surveys by, 28; nondegree alumni of, 8
Dun & Bradstreet Credit Services, 91
Dunn, J. A., Jr., 3, 62, 65, 77, 83, 87, 89

E

Education colleges, alumni research for, 70
Engineering colleges, alumni research for, 70, 73
Ewell, P. T., 71, 75, 85, 87, 89, 92
Exxon Education Foundation, 79

F

Fine Arts colleges, alumni research for, 70
Fisher, M. B., 2, 25, 38
Friends, as associate alumni, 9
Fundraising: alumni growth model for, 51-53, 62; alumni research applications for, 51-65; budget and workload indexing for, 53-54; costs of, 62; data usefulness to, 56-58, 60-61; and donor characteristics, 54-56; donor flow model for, 62; donor profiling for, 53-58; and models of giving, 82-83; prospect ranking for, 58-61, 63; research needed on, 83-84; researcher-practitioner interface for, 61; strategic planning for, 61-64; summary of, 64-65

G

General education colleges, alumni research for, 70, 71, 74
Gorman, B., 90

H

Harvard University, data analysis at, 93
Hays, J. C., 82, 86
Health and human services colleges, alumni research for, 70, 73-74

I

IBM, data analysis at, 93
Independent Sector, 2, 7
Information systems: aspects of managing, 13-23; basic records for, 15-16; computerized files for, 18; coordination of, 19-20; creating and maintaining, 20-21; current state of, 13-17; factors for successful, 14-15; hard files for, 17-18; ideal, 22-23; management of, 16-17; physical management of, 17-18; planning steps for, 18-22; resource analysis for, 20; resources on, 90-92; testing, 21-22; uses of, 15

Institutional research. *See* Alumni research
Internal Revenue Service, data analysis at, 93

K

Kerlinger, F. N., 45, 49
Klem, L., 49, 93
Kotler, P., 5, 11, 29, 38, 53–54, 65, 90

L

Lilly Endowment, 79
Litten, L., 79

M

Mail surveys, 28–29, 32–34
Maves, K. K., 2, 13, 23
Melchiori, G. S., 2, 3, 5, 6, 8, 11, 51, 59, 65, 89, 94
Michigan, University of: alumni survey by, 31, 35; clipping service for, 21; data analysis by, 47, 93; fundraising applications at, 54–56, 57, 59–60
Miller, A. F., 29, 38, 93
Moden, G. O., 2, 67, 76
Morgan, J. N., 46, 49, 93
Multiple-classification analysis (MCA), 45–46
Multiple-regression analysis, 45

N

National Association of College and University Business Officers (NACUBO), 62, 65, 78–79, 87
National Center for Accreditation of Teacher Education, 74
National Center for Higher Education Management Systems (NCHEMS), 7, 68, 76, 93

O

Ohio University: alumni board of, 73, 75; alumni research at, 68–75; background on, 68–71; funding and external evaluation at, 74–75; individual colleges at, 70, 71–74

Online services, for information systems, 91
Outcomes information, alumni research for, 9, 74–75

P

Pace, C., 67–68, 76, 90
Paton, G. J., 54, 65, 82, 87
Pedhazur, E. J., 45, 49
Periodicals, on information systems, 90
Pickett, W. L., 82, 87
Profiling: for data analysis, 44; for fundraising, 53–58
Program review, and alumni research, 9

R

Ranking: for data analysis, 44–48; of fundraising prospects, 58–61, 63
Retention studies, and alumni research, 9
Rucker, M., 30, 38

S

Sampling: for data analysis, 42; for surveys, 27–28
Segmentation, for data analysis, 42, 43–44
Social Surveys Limited, data analysis at, 93
Sonquist, J. A., 46, 49, 93
Southern California Edison, information management by, 90
Stanford University: alumni records at, 17; alumni survey by, 27
Statistical Innovations, 93
Statistical Software, 93
Strategic planning, for fundraising, 61–64
Student outcomes information, and alumni research, 9, 74–75
Surveys: aspects of, 25–38; census, 28; conclusion on, 38; costs of, 37–38; and data entry, 31–32; instruments for, 29–30; by mail, 28–29, 32–34; methods for, 26–28; package design for, 30–31; political considerations for, 25–26; polls of random samples

Surveys *(continued)*
for, 27-28; production considerations for, 31-35; publicizing, 35; resources on, 92-93; response collection for, 36-37; sample size and errors for, 27; by telephone, 28-29, 34-35; timelines for, 32
Szady, S. M., 2, 39, 50, 59

T

Telematch, 92
Telephone Lookup Service, 92
Telephone matching services, for information systems, 91-92
Telephone surveys, 28-29, 34-35
Thomas, E. G., 84, 87
Tracing services, for information systems, 92
TransUnion, 91
TRW, 91

U

U.S. Census Bureau, data analysis at, 93
U.S. Postal Service, and change of address, 21, 92

V

VU/TEXT Information Services, 91

W

Wake Forest University, telephone survey by, 34
Wealth, measurement of, 81-82
Williford, A. M., 2, 67, 76
Wogan & Associates, 92

Y

Yale University, alumni records at, 17